Dear Pastor:
If the Sheep Could Speak

Ralph V. Reynolds

Alpha Bible Publications
P.O. Box 155
Hood River, OR. 97031

***Dear Pastor:* If The Sheep Could Speak**

2nd Edition December 1989

Cover Design by Ben Bisbee

All Biblical quotes are from the King James Version unless otherwise noted.

Library of Congress Catalog Card Number: 88-82679

ISBN 1-877917-01-X

Printed in the United States of America

Dear Pastor:
If the Sheep Could Speak

Other books by Alpha Bible Publications:

By Ralph V. Reynolds

Can A Believer Be Lost?

Dividing The Word Of Truth

(also available in Spanish)

If the Sheep Could Speak

Living The Crucified Life

Making Full Proof Of Your Ministry

Portraits Of The Bride

Unbroken Vows

and the Alpha Bible Course which is widely used in the United States, Canada, and around the world.

By Leamon T. Reynolds

Love 'Em ... & Leave 'Em (an Autobiography)

By David Ward

Judgment With Mercy

The Common Salvation

The Means To Revival

By Raymond A. Sirstad

The Soulwinners Memorization Manual

For any of these books and more please write the publisher for a price list.

Dedicated to the memory of
four great Shepherds,
each of whom inspired and
influenced me in his own way,
in the early days of my ministry:

Otis A. Moore

Clarence L. Cross

Arthur Downing

Oscar Vouga

PREFACE

The first book I attempted to write was in 1953, *"Making Full Proof of Our Ministry"*. A number of years later I wrote a second ministerial book, *"All Things To All Men"*. Now I am attempting to write a third book directed to the ministry.

I do not consider myself to be an authority, and yet, after preaching the gospel for fifty-two years, I cannot be considered a novice. During these fifty-two years I have witnessed a few things which have made my heart bleed. I am convinced that there are men trying to pastor who were never called to pastor. Their main problem is that they are out of the will of God. They are a ministerial misfit. As a Christian worker in an assembly under the steady leadership of a pastor they would be a tremendous success. As a mate, second in command, their lives would be fruitful. As the captain, in charge of the ship, they only create havoc.

I write these words not to be sarcastic or critical. Instead, my heart's desire is to be helpful and to encourage each one to be a successful worker in the will of God.

Years ago I pastored a fine church in eastern Ontario for four and one half years. The young pastor who followed thought that there were many things which needed correction. This he proceeded to do. When he finished the church had divided in three ways. Another church which I turned over was completely closed and the building sold. Twelve families were scattered. I wish I could say that these two churches were the only ones which suffered in this manner, but I have witnessed this same thing being repeated too many times.

As a result I have been burdened to attempt for the third time to write a book addressed to the ministry. The theme of this book may be summed up thus: *"The shepherd leads the sheep. He does not drive them. If sheep are driven they will jump through every hole in the fence. If the shepherd leads, the sheep will follow him through dark valleys and perilous paths."*

If this book, *"Dear Pastor, If the Sheep Could Speak"* can help pastor and minister to become true shepherds, loving, leading, and willing to give their lives for the sheep, it will accomplish the purpose for which it was written.

Ralph V. Reynolds
Surrey, B.C. Canada

FOREWORD

Reverend Ralph Reynolds has had a fruitful and expansive ministry which has reached to all portions of the world. He has been a pastor. He has been a missionary in the isle of Jamaica. He has written numbers of books and Bible study courses, which have reached into the lives of countless hundreds. He has also worked in an official capacity as a District Superintendent of the United Pentecostal Church. He has been a Bible College President and is now an honorary member of the General Board of the United Pentecostal Church International.

By identifying this man's role in the oneness Pentecostal movement we bring to you a seasoned veteran of the Gospel. The many years that he has ministered successfully gives him the unusual vantage point of looking back in retrospection on the pitfalls that beset the ministry of the work of God, as well as the great successes that have been equally as experiential in his own personal life. It is specifically important to note that this is not the book of a novice. It is the book of a man who through dutiful, loyal representation of the kingdom of God has carved a niche of respectability and revered honor. The opportunity to look into the depth and the profundity of this book will give you a greater insight into the work of God through the church. Every minister and saint of God should have this book in their treasury of reading materials. Brother Reynolds brings to us not only a unique title but a very unique presentation. The title is "*Dear Pastor, If the Sheep Could Speak.*"

The relationship between the pastor and the saint of God is beautifully illustrated in his explanation of church structure. He places the pastor in the position of honor as pertains to the Scriptures. He gives an enlightening explanation of the sheep of the fold, or the saint of God, under the leadership of the pastor, as to the rights that he has to speak. All of this is couched very scripturally in a beautiful area of mutual relationship between a sheep and his shepherd.

There are lines of great wisdom that can only be gained through experience with people. Let me give a very pungent line or two. "*The work of the minister is extremely involved and complex. He must be a business executive, an architect and an organizer. However, first of all, he is called to minister to men and women. His main work is in the saving of souls.*" Let me give you another quote: "*May the sheep speak? Certainly, but never in rebellion nor in criticism of their shepherd. Sheep must never speak to sow seeds of discord and dissension in the flock. When they are guilty of such action they must be firmly disciplined and silenced. God has stated that He hates the person that sows discord among the brethren (Proverbs 6:19)."* These are a few of many lines which are of very great necessity for the ministry to understand. I am giving you these to whet your appetite.

In the furtherance of the development of the theme he discusses who is a minister, gives an excellent treatise on the body of Christ, tells why he believes in church organization, the need for the love and compassion of a shepherd, the beautiful preaching of God's Word, and how the voice of God is heard and where its proper focus lies.

This book is desperately needed in these days. The cacophony of voices that are being heard in our present world are confusing to the ears of Christians, and it is difficult for them to hear what "thus saith the Spirit to the church". Brother Reynolds, in his unique manner, has captured the essence of proper relationships between pastor and congregation. He also adds the years of his observation of the ministry into excellent advice. Today, as in no other era, men who are called to shepherd the sheep have been misdirected by luring affluence, subtle temptations, serious snares, unlooked-for opposition, and false accusations. Because of this confused climate existing in our times this book gives clear insight into what is important as far as the work of the man of God is concerned.

I have read much of this outstanding treatise on this subject and, I confess, reread some of it several times. I heartily recommend this book to every born-again child of God, to every prospective minister, to every pastor, every evangelist and every teacher. None of us have so many years of experience of such a wealth of knowledge that we cannot be taught. This book teaches. It directs. It opens doors of new thought and it confirms the true way of pastoral guidance. To pay for this kind of spiritual insight and discernment into delicate areas of the ministry and their proper relationship to the sheep of God's pasture, takes a man of the stature of Ralph Reynolds.

You will find yourself as I found myself, nodding affirmation to the many blessed instructions. You will also find yourself looking into a mirror and seeing your own self under similar circumstances. If you are a novice in the work of the Lord this book will serve the purpose of lighting your pathway for the future.

This book teaches ethics, which in some instances is being trodden underfoot because unethical men do not care for righteousness. It teaches a deep sense of compassion and concern for people. It also teaches saints of God to recognize ministerial authority in a proper recognition. The book does not over balance either side of the shepherd or the sheep. It cuts a straight path through all the numerous issues that develop in a local assembly or in an international church body.

It is with the utmost of confidence that I write this

foreword in behalf of a splendid man who has labored tirelessly, who has blessed the Pentecostal movement for several decades, who still lives to sound out a voice of clarity in a time of chaotic confusion. Those of you who have the privilege of reading this book will agree with what I say in this foreword and perhaps will say, "Brother, you should have said more than that!"

Nathaniel A. Urshan
General Superintendent
United Pentecostal Church

TABLE OF CONTENTS

CHAPTER
ONE

DEAR PASTOR

Dear Pastor:

Greetings in the name of Jesus!

I am writing this letter because I believe that I can express myself better in written word than in speech. I believe that you can help for there are some things that trouble me concerning the ministry. I realize that I am doing wrong in judging a minister of the gospel, at any time. However, my confidence has been shaken at times, and I certainly want to keep a strong faith in the men of

God who preach to me.

Pastor, I sincerely thank God for you. In you, I have complete confidence and trust. You have faithfully ministered God's Word and are truly a man of God at all times. What we see in the pulpit is also the man that we see in your home or at the supermarket. At all times, you live what you preach. For this reason, I love and trust you. For this same reason, I feel I can write you this letter knowing that I can trust you with the doubts and fears that I frequently encounter.

When we sit in church, we are part of a captive audience. We are expected to accept and believe everything we hear. There is no way that we can even ask for clarification or further explanation. As born-again Christians filled with the Holy Ghost, we still have the ability to think for ourselves. We are not puppets but human beings, breathing and very much alive. We are intelligent beings, still capable of making decisions and choices for ourselves. Surely we are more than a bunch of gullible non-entities.

May I illustrate to explain my dilemma: I have heard a minister say that when he preached his voice was that of God. Pastor, I can willingly accept that he is God's spokesman, a commissioned ambassador speaking on behalf of God, but to claim that his voice was that of the Lord, I cannot accept. I have heard too many incorrect things spoken by the ministry and seen too many errors. God never makes a mistake and is infallible. The minister is a God-anointed preacher of the gospel, but he is still human. My desire is to respect him and listen to him with confidence, but extravagant statements like this shock me to the roots of my being.

Also, I am sorry to say I have seen too many examples of a double standard. To preach one thing and to practice something absolutely contradictory is mere hypocrisy. If you request it, I can give you many examples. Finally, Pastor, may I ask a question that has troubled me. Are there two bodies: one for the ministry and another for the laity? Are there two Holy Spirits: one for the preacher and another for the saints? Is it not the same Holy Spirit which speaks to both the saints and the pastor? I certainly would appreciate your comments regarding this. Are the sheep only expected to listen? What would happen if the sheep could speak? I am certain that many things would change!

I shall be looking forward to your reply and would be happy to meet you in the church office or my home. If you prefer, you may answer me by writing. Whatever you do, I know that it will help me and quiet many of my apprehensions and fears. Although frequently troubled in mind and soul, I trust you will believe that I am still one of your faithful sheep. May the Lord bless you richly!

With sincere prayers,

Joe.

CHAPTER TWO

DEAR JOE

Dear Brother Joe:

Greetings! Yesterday, I received your letter and am giving you an immediate reply.

I appreciate your frankness and honesty and shall certainly try to help you with some of your problems. I am sufficiently concerned that I am taking the time to deal with the entire matter existing between the shepherd and his flock. After you have prayerfully read the enclosed chapters relating to the ministry, communicate with me.

We shall then make an appointment to discuss the problems that are troubling you.

However, in this letter, I shall draw your attention to two important principles. First of all, there are spiritual, victorious saints, and also cold, carnal, defeated, professing ones, and many who are at varying degrees of spirituality in between those two extremes. It is wrong to judge all Christians by looking at the worldly believers. Each one must be judged separately, on his own merit. Likewise, there are successful ministers of the gospel, those who have failed, and those who have succeeded or failed in various degrees between these two extremes. It definitely is wrong to lose faith in the ministry because of one or two who have made mistakes. It could be that some of these have failed because they are attempting to do what God has never called them to do. As a result, they are frustrated and discouraged, in need of encouragement not harsh censorship.

The second principle to consider is that the sheep listen to the voice of the shepherd. It is he who speaks and leads. The sheep know his voice and follow him (John 10:27). It is the shepherd's responsibility to lead and the sheep's to be willing to follow. When this divine law is broken and the order reversed, the flock is in severe trouble. The shepherd must be in front leading. When the sheep are in front of the shepherd, he attempts to drive. When this happens, the sheep will jump through every hole in the fence they can find, and are scattered.

This does not mean that there are not times when the sheep should have the privilege to speak. At such times, the shepherd listens to determine the need of the flock. By doing this, he can determine if they are hungry, weak, straying sheep to whom he must give immediate attention. However, the decision-making prerogative is still firmly in the shepherd's hands. He leads them to the pasture to feed them and by the springs and streams to water them. He keeps away the wild animals and protects them against dangers that could destroy the flock.

Is it permissible for the sheep to speak? Certainly, but only if they are at the same time listening to the voice of the shepherd and following their God-ordained leader. If their voice is raised in contradiction to the voice of the shepherd and they attempt to lead, havoc and tragedy are the results.

Joe, I thank you for your sincerity and honesty. After you have read these studies on pastoral duties and relationship, contact me. We shall deal with the matter fully until every doubt and apprehension are gone.

With sincere prayers,

Pastor.

CHAPTER THREE

WHO IS A SAINT?

"To all that be in Rome, beloved of God, called to be saints ..." (Romans 1:7).

In the Old Testament, the root words which are translated "saints" express holiness and godliness. The basic meaning seems to be "a separation unto God." In the New Testament the word is used frequently, and the meaning is synonymous with that of being a believer. To be a saint does not mean that a person is wearing a halo or has sprouted wings; however, it does mean that the saint is a member of the body of Christ, separated from the world and called to be Christ-like.

To be a saint does not mean that one has to be so super spiritual that he makes himself obnoxious wherever he is. It is true that he is spiritually minded; but at the same time, he understands that he lives in a world of reality.

It has been said that a professing believer is either a "saint" or an "ain't". Certainly, every Christian desires to be a successful and true saint. No one wants to be an "ain't".

Who actually is a saint? Who are these sheep who are members of the Lord's flock? Well, let us attempt to clearly identify a saint, one of His precious saints for whom Jesus died.

First of all, he is a human being, a breathing and living person. No two people are exactly alike. He is an individual in his own right, with his own personality. He possesses his own feelings and emotions and can be tempted with discouragement. He can experience loneliness and frustration, and long for understanding and love. As a human being, he is an intelligent creature with ability to make decisions. As a free-will agent, he is responsible for making his own choices.

Secondly, he is a Christian, a born-again child of God. He has repented, been baptized in Jesus' name, and filled with the Holy Spirit. As a son of God, he is a member of God's family, a brother and sister of all of God's children.

Regardless of his age, sex, or race, he is one of God's own.

Thirdly, he is a member of the body of Christ. He has been baptized into the body by the Holy Spirit (I Corinthians 12:13). He has been placed in the body where it has pleased God. It makes no difference the position he holds for all are important. There is no such thing as an unimportant, insignificant member of the body. His presence in the body is essential. When he is not there, the body is lacking a vital part. The health and growth of the body is dependent upon the health and growth of every member (Ephesians 4:16). Therefore, it is necessary that the child of God be a "saint", not just a professing "ain't".

As a member of the body of Christ, he must give his love, loyalty, and allegiance to Jesus Christ. In fact, Jesus must come first in his heart and mind at all times. Second to Jesus, comes his love and loyalty to his spouse and family. Next ranks a saint's love for his pastor, the God-ordained shepherd who watches over his soul. If he has his priorities right, there will never be a tug of war in his heart, pulling two or more different ways. Jesus will always be number one, the wife or husband will be number two, and the man of God who feeds his soul will be number three. Everything else will fall in the proper place if the saint keeps a correct relationship between the church and home.

It should be understood that no two saints will be identical. Each will be a little different.

Although the saint will be following the example of the

shepherd, his life must be patterned at all times after that of Christ. Christ-likeness should be his goal. When one's life is patterned after Christ's, he will be an example of a victorious, spiritual saint but at the same time maintain the distinctiveness of his own individuality and personality. Cloning is never to be desired. However, only too frequently, this is the unhappy result when a Christian patterns after a man.

Years ago I attended the Outlet camp meeting in Ontario. During the testimony service a number of Christians stood and testified, almost everyone in the same manner. After listening, I decided that they were from one church which was located out of the province. After the service I enquired where these saints were from. I was not surprised to hear that I was correct in my belief. In my estimation, the difficulty here was that clones were being produced, not spiritual saints with their own individuality.

When cloning takes place, the imperfections are invariably copied too. Going back to those years of which I have just mentioned, I sat under the ministry of a world renowned evangelist who left an impression upon me as a young preacher. I noticed as he walked across the platform, he would straighten out one leg and drag it behind him. Not long after, I found that during my preaching I was doing the same thing, mimicking the evangelist. When I awakened to my error, you may rest assured that I did not do it again. Certainly, saints are not clones, but individuals in their own right.

Should saints be poured into a mold and come out stereotyped on an assembly line? There is little said in its favor. It is certainly not glorifying the Lord.

A shepherd succeeds in disciplining the new converts when he plants the love for holiness and God's Word in their hearts. Saints are people who decide for themselves. God never removes from one the prerogative of being a free-will agent. The shepherd only succeeds when the saint lives a holy life of his own choice.

In raising a family, parents are not successful until they teach their children to meet and solve the problems of life for themselves. They are successful when the children are able to enter society and establish successful Christian homes of their own. The real test comes after the son or daughter leaves home. Likewise, the real test comes when the saint moves from the shelter of the sheepfold where he was tenderly raised and taught by the loving shepherd.

Should the sheep be allowed to speak? They must be allowed to express themselves if they are to develop and become strong saints. If they are chocked and muzzled, they will always remain weak and immature. The freedom of expression granted must never be a license to censor the pastor and cause division in the flock. It should only be granted to build and strengthen the work of God.

The saints are members of the body of Christ. They should share a mutual concern and burden for the work of God. They should pray and travail for souls. They should be faithful in church attendance and financial support. They should hold up their pastor's hands and give him strong, loyal support. If this be so, are they transgressing if they desire to express themselves? No! If their motivation is pure and spirit is right, the sheep will only speak to amen the voice of the shepherd and to encourage all to follow the wise leadership of the man of God.

CHAPTER
FOUR

WHO IS A MINISTER?

"But it shall not be so among you:: but whosoever will be great among you, let him be your minister; and whosoever will be chief among you, let him be your servant: even as the Son of man came not to be ministered unto, but to minister, and to give his life a ransom for many" (Matthew 20:26-28).

Who is a minister? The correct answer to this question is given by our Lord Himself. He defines the office of the ministry in reply to the request of James and John that they might sit on His left or right hand in His kingdom. Jesus rebuked them for this carnal desire and told them if they wanted to be great in the kingdom, they must be a servant to all.

According to our Lord, a minister is a servant. As such, he no longer thinks of his own needs but the needs of others. His time and energy are taken up with helping, encouraging and lifting up others. His main work is to minister to the saints and to serve others.

The request of the two disciples came because of a wrong motive, a perverted ambition to excel and be great in the kingdom. There is nothing wrong with ambition, but it must be pure, to exalt Christ and not self. Why do many ministers grow discouraged and quit? Is it not because of a wrong concept of the ministry. If the minister has a right understanding of the work unto which he has been called, he will seldom be discouraged. He will understand just what it means to be successful and will never set before him unrealistic goals.

He is called to be a servant and minister to the saints. The church is not there to minister to him but rather he to the church. He is their minister and a servant of the Lord to feed, strengthen, and edify the body of Christ. Some may feel that the church is to minister to the pastor, but that concept is incorrect. The Apostle Paul states that the ministry is given to the church to perform three functions: 1)To perfect the saints; 2) To perform the work of the ministry; and 3) To edify the body of Christ (Ephesians 4:12). The welfare of the saints is always uppermost in the mind of the true minister. He fully dedicates himself to watching over the flock and tending the sheepfold. This ministry is most demanding and time consuming. It is a 24 hour job, seven days a week. A minister may attempt to keep one day a week for himself and his family, but it is very difficult to succeed here. In the middle of the night or in the early hours of the morning, he can be called to the emergency ward to pray for and minister to others. Many nights when he is ready to drop with weariness, he must sit by the bedside of a sick and dying saint. He considers not his own self nor his needs but the needs of others.

Jesus fitly describes this sacrificial service of love by referring to Himself: *"I am the good shepherd: the good shepherd giveth his life for the sheep" (John 10:11). "... I lay down my life for the sheep" (John 10:15).*

It is suitable now to ask the heart searching question: Do the sheep lay down their lives for the shepherd or does the shepherd lay down his life for the sheep? there can be only one correct answer. When the sheep learn to love, respect, and follow the shepherd, undoubtedly, they are willing to lay down their lives for the shepherd. But that is not God's order! The shepherd giveth his life for the sheep.

His whole life is sacrificial and entirely expendable for the sheep. His time, talent, strength, and ability are all dedicated towards achieving the one goal of a strong, healthy, spiritual and victorious church.

The work of the minister is extremely involved and

complex. He must be a business executive, an architect and an organizer. However, first of all, he is called to minister to men and women. His main work is in the saving of souls. He is not called to build churches. There is no verse of Scripture which commissions the ministry to build large church buildings. He is not called to conduct fund raising drives nor is he called to have ambitious expansion programs and mortgage the lives of the next generation. His calling is simple and clearly defined. He is called to be a servant. His office is one of responsibility rather than that of privilege.

God's method is that of ministering through God called ministers. It is not bigger and better church buildings nor more and better programs that are desperately needed to bring revival in the sunset hours of this church age. The need is currently for that of better ministers, men and women dedicated to giving their lives for others. Dying, if needful, that others may live.

The church can never go farther nor reach higher than that reached by the faithful laborers of her ministry.

The minister is a saint's best friend apart from Jesus Himself. He is a counselor who will listen and understand. He is the leader who will go before the flock, leading them in paths of righteousness and holiness. He not only faithfully teaches, admonishes and instructs but personally demonstrates what it means to be a Christian, a victorious saint standing solemnly for truth and holiness.

Do the sheep need to speak when they have a true shepherd? Why should they want to speak? If they do speak, what have they to say? God has given them a shepherd to watch over their souls and lead them from earth to glory. Our Lord teaches that it is the shepherd who speaks and the sheep know His voice and follow.

CHAPTER
FIVE

THE BODY OF CHRIST

"And hath put all things under his feet, and gave him to be the head over all things to the church, which is his body, the fulness of him that filleth all in all" (Ephesians 1:22-23).

Jesus told His disciples that it was necessary for Him to go away for if He did not go away, the Comforter would not come (John 16:7). What actually did Jesus mean by this statement? The Holy Ghost was here present when He spoke these words. John the Baptist had been filled with the Holy Ghost from birth. The Lord's own Father was the

Holy Ghost (Matthew 1:20).

At Pentecost, God did a brand new thing. The church was born a living, pulsating organism, a body indwelt by Jesus Christ Himself. Thus the church was born to be the body of Christ upon the earth. Before His Ascension, Jesus dwelt upon earth in the body which was conceived in the womb of the virgin. Since Pentecost Jesus has dwelt upon earth in the body which was born in the Upper Room. The church has become His feet, His hands, His voice upon earth. Now it can be understood why it was necessary for Jesus to leave before the Comforter could come. The mystery that has been hid for ages is no longer a mystery. The Holy Ghost has taken upon Himself a new office which is Christ in the church, the hope of glory. *"To whom God would make known what is the riches of the glory of this mystery among the Gentiles; which is Christ in you, the hope of glory" (Colossians 1:27).*

Upon this established fact another important truth may now be stated: There is only one church; there is only one body (Ephesians 4:4). God is one, not a plurality. We have only one Lord (Ephesians 4:4). There are not and never can be two bodies of Christ. There is not one body for the sheep and another for the shepherd. *"For by one Spirit are we all baptized into one body ..." (I Corinthians 12:13).* We are all placed into the body by the same experience of Holy Ghost baptism. We are all members one of another. As members of the body of Christ, whether we be ministers or laity, we have become recipients of the same Holy Spirit, and the same life is pulsating through each of us.

Although every believer is a member of the one and same body, not every member has the same office. Everyone is not called to perform the same work nor to occupy the same place of responsibility. The body will be healthy, strong and virile when each member is functioning in his God-ordained place. Not everyone can be the leader, the organist nor the Sunday School Superintendent. However, God has placed everyone in the body according to their ability, talent and capability. When all are content in their God ordained place and have dedicated themselves to the task allotted to them, beautiful unity and harmony exists within the body. When this occurs, the body grows and expands naturally, without strain nor stress. It should be kept in mind that the Christian can always successfully do the work God has called him to do. If God has called him to be an usher, he can do the job well. The Lord will never call one to do a job for which he is not capable of doing. With the call of God, always comes the strength, power, grace and knowledge necessary to function within the body in a healthy manner.

The trouble comes when one desires to occupy a place he had never been called to. When this happens, it inevitable ends in tragic failure. When the member of the body tries to fulfill a calling that is out of the will of God, he encounters frustrations, discouragement and failure. The will of God can always be done and done successfully. God will never place one of His children in a position of frustration and defeat.

The important thing to always remember is to be content

wherever God places you and to do what task God has assigned to you with joy and enthusiasm. Happiness and success will always be the result. When a saint tries to occupy a place of responsibility out of the will of God, the whole body suffers. The saint should never allow himself to be motivated with envy or carnal ambition. Diotrephes loved the preeminence and brought division (III John 9). A situation like this within the body is a cancer which must be removed, if need be by a painful surgery.

Both the ministry and laity are members of the same body. Both have been recipients of and are lead by the same Spirit. However, both have not been called to the same work. One has been called to lead, the other to follow. One has been called to speak, the other to listen to his shepherd's voice.

Is it permissible for the sheep to speak? Certainly, but only in the place in the body where God has placed him. He speaks as a member of the body, as one of the flock, but never as the shepherd leading the flock. When the pastor is a good shepherd and each member is a good saint, functioning as members one of the other, the body is healthy and grows and grows and grows (Ephesians 4:16).

CHAPTER
SIX

CHURCH ORGANIZATION

"And God hath set some in the church, first apostles, secondarily prophets, thirdly teachers, after that miracles, then gifts of healings, helps governments, diversities of tongues" (I Corinthians 12:28).

Some people profess that they do not believe in organization in the church; however, they certainly believe in organization elsewhere. What kind of home would they have without definite order? What kind of traffic would there be in our cities without traffic laws? Without proper organization, all would be in confusion. But God is not the author of such. *"For God is not the author of confusion, but of peace, as in all churches of the saints " (I Corinthians 14:33).*

The man who has driven his car into the ditch during a snow storm certainly believes in organization when some assistance comes. Four men can push an automobile out of a snowbank easier than one can do it alone. This is what organization is all about. It is simply a means towards a desired end. The church is commissioned to evangelize the whole world. Certainly, by joining forces in an orderly manner; we can do more than by everyone trying to do his own thing in his own way.

There is order in everything God has done. He has always worked according to definite laws. He has a plan for the entire universe, including the church.

We see perfect order and harmony in our own physical bodies. When one member of the body is not functioning properly, the person becomes a sick man or woman. When a person is well, every member is in its proper place and functioning in a healthy manner. Such order we should always find in the church.

The church is a living organism, a spiritual body in which the presence of Christ dwells. It is not an organization but an organism. Yet, in that organism, there must be proper organization. The essential truth to be emphasized here is that the organization is within the body, not without. If we were to recognize the organization as outside the body, then we would have an organized government controlling the church from outside her own borders. This would mean that the organization would become a labor union, no more no less. God has placed within the church administrations (I Corinthians 12:28). The organization is certainly not a labor union or a bureaucracy dictating to the body. Christ dwells within the body and administers from within. This means that every office and governmental position is also placed within the body.

I repeat that this principle is important and should be understood by every member of the church.

Every member of the church needs a God ordained pastor, a shepherd who watches over his spiritual welfare. In turn, every pastor needs a pastor, a God ordained leader to whom he is answerable. Here we see the need for the district and international structure of our church.

God places every member in the body as it hath pleased Him (I Corinthians 12:18). Beautiful harmony exists when every member functions where he is placed. He does his best in the role where God has called him and faithfully supports those whom God has placed over him. When this happens, there is no division in the body (I Corinthians 12:25). Everyone, both shepherd and sheep, may feel free to express himself but always for the welfare of the whole body.

I have heard men state that they do not want a church

board. I personally will not pastor a church without one. However, the board of deacons or trustees work under the leadership of their pastor. Reverse this, and there is trouble. The board is always responsible to the pastor, not vice versa. God's order always brings about strength and harmony.

The Apostle Paul shows the importance of every member of the body functioning properly and relates this condition to the growth of the body (Ephesians 4:16). With God's planned order and administration within the body, the church will experience revival and growth.

I personally am suspicious of every independent preacher and layman. I am fearful of every independent spirit. We all need one another, and together we need divine direction from God Himself.

Do I believe in organization? I certainly do because organization is of God. Let me give you five reasons why I know that this is so:

1. Scriptures state that God has placed administration in the body (I Corinthians 12:28);
2. God is not a God of confusion but of order;
3. The independent spirit is basically the spirit of rebellion;
4. All nature testifies that God is a God of organization and order;
5. Without organization, life as we know it could not continue.

I believe in organization because it brings harmony and peace, strength and revival. Organization permits us to unite together to do the great work that God has called us to, the evangelism of the lost world.

CHAPTER
SEVEN

THE SHEEPFOLD

"My sheep hear my voice, and I know them, and they follow me" (John 10:27).

In the tenth chapter of the gospel of St. John, Jesus gave us a beautiful picture of the church. Here He likened the saints unto sheep, securely resting each night within a sheepfold and each morning led out to pasture by the shepherd of the flock. In this rich lesson, our Lord called Himself the good shepherd and identified Himself as such by the qualification of giving His life for the sheep.

Each local church assembly is a sheepfold. Each pastor is an under shepherd working under the direction of the chief shepherd or good shepherd (I Peter 5:4). Each born again believer is a sheep or lamb within the flock. The main qualification of being a shepherd is that he is willing to die for the sheep. The qualification of being a sheep is that he knows his shepherd's voice and follows him.

The sheepfold was an enclosure under the open sky, fenced by a stone wall or a thick brush. In each case, the fence was designed and built to give security. The sheep could not wander outside and the predators could not get inside to destroy. Frequently, several flocks would be sheltered throughout the night within one sheepfold. One shepherd would watch over the entire flock during the night and in the morning, the shepherd would come and call his sheep to the gate. The sheep of his flock would know his voice and come running. They would pass under his rod as he counted. After his entire flock had answered the call of his voice, he would lead them to the pasture.

It is important to clearly understand that the shepherd lead them to pasture and the sheep followed. If he tried to drive the sheep, they would scatter. Sheep which are driven will jump through every hole in the fence. Another truth which must be understood is that the sheep do not choose the pasture. The decision regarding where they will feed is the shepherd's responsibility.

The care and safety of the sheep are always that of the shepherd. They are secure and healthy when they keep close to their shepherd; they are harmed and destroyed when they wander away. They are especially in a perilous situation when they are beyond hearing the shepherd's voice. It is important to always remember that it is the shepherd who speaks, not the sheep. The sheep listen and follow.

Before they can follow, they must know the shepherd's voice. Years ago, I read a story told by a minister who had travelled in the East. He came to a shepherd watching over a flock of sheep. He listened to the shepherd as he called his sheep and watched as they responded to his voice. He approached the shepherd and asked how he might be able to call the sheep. The shepherd tried to persuade him that it was of no use to try because they knew not his voice and would not respond. But the visitor insisted he wanted to try. The shepherd knew that this was totally in vain, but after much persuasion, the shepherd agreed to change clothes with the visitor. The shepherd told the foreigner just exactly what to say and even tried to help him with the accent of each word. The visitor approached the sheep and called them. They continued to feed. Not one of them responded; after several attempts, he gave up. Then the shepherd, even though he was dressed in strange garb, spoke to the sheep; they lifted their heads and came running to him. They knew his voice; the voice of the stranger they did not know.

The heart of the shepherd is the key of being a successful pastor. If the sheep are to trust, love, respect and follow him, he must prove that he is a God called shepherd by attending the flock with love and gentleness. The respect and authority which belongs to the pastor must be earned and not demanded. If he loves the saints, they will love him in return. If he shows them respect, they will honor him with their respect. If he inspires confidence, they will obey him. This is a time consuming relationship, and the pastor must not become impatient.

In my own experience, it takes three years to become a pastor. When he is installed in this office by the District Superintendent, he is, of course, officially the pastor of that particular assembly. However, he actually is not really the shepherd until he is fully accepted, and the sheep fully recognize the voice of their shepherd. This takes time. Many churches are torn up by a new minister prematurely trying to make drastic changes which the people resent. By waiting until he is in the driver's seat and all know that he is their leader under God, he is able to keep the church united and strong. At that time, he is able to introduce policies and carry them through to a successful conclusion. This he would never be able to do when he was a newly installed pastor.

Every saint needs to be a member of a local assembly and have a church home. Every sheep should know the sheepfold to which he belongs. Every believer should have a pastor, and every sheep a shepherd. It is a dangerous thing to be uprooted and adrift. There are many enemies which would rob and destroy the sheep. Thieves, robbers and hirelings would scatter the flock and leave them wounded and bleeding. Every Christian must attend church faithfully and be under the watchful care of a loving pastor who has a shepherd's heart.

After accepting the call to pastor a church assembly where I had previously pastored, I naturally looked for all the members of the flock. Upon enquiry, I learned that a certain family had left the church and were not attending anywhere. Not long afterward, I met this sister upon the street. I greeted her and told her how I missed her and then enquired where she and her husband were attending church. "Oh," she replied, "We do not go to church anymore. God told us that we could stay home and worship there. Here we have our church and do not go out to worship."

This sister lied to me! For God has told no one to absent himself from the church. *"Not forsaking the assembling of ourselves together, as the manner of some is; but exhorting one another and so much the more as ye see the day approaching" (Hebrews 10:25).* God never tells a person to do something which is contrary to His Word.

The benefits of having a church home are many. Here within the sheepfold is security, safety and the loving care of a true shepherd. Here he is fed the Word of God, and his soul is fed with the finest of the wheat. He can drive down his roots and feel the sense of belonging. Here he can enjoy the fellowship of the saints and feel himself growing and becoming stronger each day.

The sheepfold is God's order. His plan is that every child of His should have a church home, attend faithfully, and grow spiritually strong under the watchful eye of a loving shepherd.

CHAPTER
EIGHT

WANDERING SHEEP

"And when he hath found it, he layeth it on his shoulder, rejoicing. And when he cometh home, he called together his friends and neighbors, saying unto them, Rejoice with me; for I have found my sheep which was lost" (Luke 15:5-6).

Years ago in Jamaica, I asked a Bible class which was more important: to save a sinner or to keep a converted believer in the church? An elder who pastored a Pentecostal church in the city answered, "It is more important to save a sinner, to win a new convert." When he was asked for a Scripture to justify his answer, he replied, saying that Jesus taught the parable of the shepherd with the hundred sheep in the wilderness. The shepherd left the ninety and nine to find the one lost sheep.

"But," I replied, "the one hundredth lost one was a sheep that had wandered away from the fold."

We are commissioned to reach the lost with the message of salvation, and every man has the right to hear the gospel. However, it is essential to feed and nourish the newborn lamb and keep him within the safety of the fold.

We must never lose sight of the fact that a wandering sheep is a backslider, and a backslider is a lost soul. The prodigal son was both lost and dead as far as the father was concerned as long as he remained in the pig's sty. The beautiful thing about this parable is that he came to himself and returned home. Wandering sheep may be found and brought back to the fold.

As a young minister, I was shocked at the statement of another young preacher. He actually boasted of the "back door" revival he had at a certain church.

A backdoor revival, is there such a thing? What could this possibly be? The term is a contradiction. If there should be a back door exodus out of an assembly, it certainly could not be called a revival. A funeral would be a better way to describe what was happening. Those precious people who were walking out of the back door were going to be wandering sheep, backsliders, lost and dying souls.

The ministry of the shepherd is to save the assembly from such a heart rending experience. As a pastor, I have lost my share of souls. At one time, I lost eight families from the church. It hurt and my heart pained. However, I did not try to appease my feelings by harshly censoring those straying sheep. I searched my heart and asked myself where I had failed? Why was I not able to help them in their need and keep them in the fold? The thing that concerned the heart of this pastor was not where had they failed, but rather, where had I failed.

The ministry of any church is to save the lost and keep them saved in the church.

A preacher once asked this question: "Is the church a saved fellowship or a saving fellowship?" Of course, a correct answer to this question is that the church is both. In order to be saved, we must be in the church. However, the saints are the salt of the earth. If they are weak and sick lambs, they should be ministered to. The dedication and spirituality of the older sheep should be able to overcome the weakness of the young lambs who have just been added to the fold. There should be no fear in having weak ones in the church who need teaching and nourishment.

In fact, if the perfect church assembly could be found, they would need no pastor. For in this case, his work would be completed. The work and ministry of the shepherd is clearly within the church. The Apostle Paul clearly defines his ministry as being thus: 1) To perfect; 2) To minister; and 3) To build up the saints (Ephesians 4:12). One of the great ministries of the saints is to restore the weak (Galatians 6:1). This he must always do in the spirit of meekness, knowing that he could himself be overtaken with a fault.

The fact that the Lord has placed within the body the nine gifts of the Spirit is proof that the church is not perfect. Each of the gifts of the Spirit is manifested upon demand as there is need. How could the gift of the word of wisdom or the word of knowledge be manifested if there were no problems in the church? How could the gifts of healing be manifested if there was no sickness? How could the gift of discerning of spirits be manifested if there werc no wrong spirits? The fact that the Lord has placed within the church the nine gifts of the Spirit is proof that many times the church is in need of help.

In the parable of the sower found in Matthew 13, Jesus taught that the seed would be sown upon various types of soil. Because of this, there may be people within an assembly with wayside hearts, stoney hearts, thorny hearts, and hearts with good soil as well. People are people. There are all kinds. Everyone has the right to hear the gospel, and the preacher must minister to them regardless of the response. His capability to minister will not be measured by his ability to minister only to those that bear one hundred fold, but rather, he will be judged by his ability to minister to the stoney and thorny ground hearers, also. Can he help them? This must be his burden and concern.

Within the walls of the church, there will be those who will be classified as being "tares". However, Jesus taught that we should leave the tares alone. If we pull them up, we shall pull up some of the wheat along with them.

There is a note of warning that must be given. The welfare of the individual must never have priority over the welfare of the whole body. In every assembly there comes a time when the true pastor must use discipline. For the good of the flock, there occasionally comes a time when an eradication must take place, as painful as it may be.

Here are some classes that must be dealt with: 1) The heretic after the second admonition (Titus 3:10); 2) The one who causes division (Romans 16:17); and 3) The immoral who commits incest (I Corinthians 5:11). Jesus taught that if one refuses to be reconciled, he is to become an heathen and a publican (Matthew 18:15-17).

In each case of discipline, it is done with sorrow and always for the welfare of the church. Never is discipline administered or people disfellowshipped on a personal basis. Never should it become a personal confrontation between the pastor and a member of the congregation. It is always with a bleeding heart and after all other means have failed that one is disfellowshipped.

He will do his upmost to win them and keep them within

the fold. As long as they are attending the church, there is hope that they can be helped. They may be worldly, carnal and cold spiritually, but I shall do my best to keep them attending church. I would rather preach to some backsliders than to empty benches. I get more inspiration by ministering to people than to an empty church.

It has been said by some that they must have a clean church. Well, dust off the benches and vacuum off the carpets, and you may have a clean church but an empty one.

As for me, give me people to preach to. People with weaknesses, faults, and yes, their sins. Ones who are tempted, discouraged, lonely, and frustrated. People who need help, restless, uneasy, and dissatisfied. Ones who may be backsliders, wandering from the fold. Give me the opportunity to search for them in the wilderness, to look them up in the middle of the night or in the early morning, at home or on the job. Here, in this way, the ministry of the church is expressed.

What happens when a church has a revival? The backsliders, the wandering sheep, make their way back home first. After that, miracles take place. Strangers make their way to the church where they find love and compassion. Coming out of a cold, harsh world of sin, they make their way to the foot of the cross. At the altar of the church the shepherd tenderly cares for all of the sheep, the sick and the weak as well as the strong and healthy.

CHAPTER
NINE

BACK DOOR REVIVAL

"But he said, Nay; lest while ye gather up the tares, ye root up also the wheat with them" (Matthew 13:29).

There is no such thing as a back door revival. The term is contradictory. It is certainly not a revival when there is an exodus out of the church. A revival is a time of renewal and refreshing; the saints are revived and encouraged. Backsliders are reclaimed, and miracles take place. As a direct result of this revival, there is an increase of the body. Sinners enter the church and are delivered. There is a constant increase in numbers.

Jesus taught in the parable of the tares that the weak and carnal ones should be kept in the church. Separation will take place on the Day of Judgment. Until then, keep them in the fold. If one attempts to uproot them, in all probability some of the wheat will be uprooted, also.

God's plan is that His house would be filled with people. This means that sometimes it is necessary to bring in the poor, the maimed, the halt and the blind (Luke 14:21). In the church, there must be no discrimination or degradation. Young and old, rich and poor, learned and ignorant, saint and sinner are encouraged to worship together. People of all races, color and culture are given a warm welcome and made to feel at home. In God's house, no one is given the cold shoulder nor slighted. A friendly smile and a warm handshake are for each one, without partiality.

The Lord's plan is that we could go into the streets and highways and compel them to come in. Sometimes just an invitation is not enough; we must compel them to come in that the Lord's house may be filled (Luke 14:23). However, it is not enough to fill up the benches with visitors and strangers. We must give them personal attention and see them pray through at the altar. Even that is not enough. They must stay in the church with their problems, struggles, and difficulties. Deliverance and restoration are the two words that apply here.

If there is a weak believer, he finds strength in the house of the Lord. If there is one that has stumbled and fallen, he finds restoration. In the sheepfold, there is continual encouragement, and the ministry of restoration is demonstrated constantly. *"Brethren, if a man be overtaken in a fault, ye which are spiritual, restore such an one in the spirit of meekness; considering thyself, lest thou also be tempted" (Galatians 6:1).* This admonition of Paul's to the Galatian church tells us that our work is one of restoration. The true shepherd never gives harsh criticism, throws stones, or pushes one who is spiritually crippled out the back door. Keeping this in mind, it must be noted that the faithful pastor must administer discipline occasionally. This is only done with the aching heart and in the spirit of love, endeavoring to save that embattled soul.

In administering discipline, the shepherd must always consider the transgression in the following order:

1. How it effects the whole church. The health and welfare of the entire body must always be the first considered.
2. The next consideration must be the restoration of the fallen believer. Sin can never be ignored; it must always be dealt with. The disciplinary action that will bring repentance and restoration must always be considered. The salvation of souls must always have first priority.
3. The feelings of the pastor himself is the last factor to influence his decision. The pastor may feel hurt and indignant; however, his own feeling must never control his action.

There are many options open to the pastor in dealing with the erring member of the church. They might be briefly mentioned here:

1. Admonition. In the pastor's office or in the brother's home, the pastor may admonish the transgressing believer.
2. Rebuke. A stern and severe rebuke may be necessary. A rebuke which is given in the Spirit is generally quite effective. This may be given privately or publicly.
3. Probation. In this act, the transgressor is silenced from the church for a definite period of time. His membership is placed under question and even suspended during this time. the length of time can vary from one month to one year.
4. Disfellowship. Keeping in mind that the main purpose of discipline is the restoration of a fallen believer, the act of disfellowship should be only used in extreme cases.
5. Handing over to Satan. This is a Scriptural form of discipline, but again, it should be used with the thought of bringing the transgressor to repentance (I Corinthians 5:5).

Dependant upon the nature of sin, the pastor must decide whether to deal with the matter 1) privately, 2) before the board of deacons, or 3) publicly before the entire church assembly. Consideration must be given to the seriousness of the matter and whether or not the church assembly knows about the problem and is suffering because of it. In such matters, a private disposition in the affair is not sufficient.

While we are considering discipline, it might be well to list some rules to be remembered:

1. The welfare of the whole body comes first. One rotten apple can spoil the whole barrel.
2. The welfare of the individual concerned comes before personal consideration.
3. In case of dispute, the pastor must hear both sides of the story. He must get all the facts, keep notes, and write down everything that has a bearing upon the problems. He should never jump to conclusions or be influenced by emotions. He should never comment about the matter until he is certain he has made the right decision.
4. The pastor must never attempt to discipline a person until he knows that he can enforce it. Once he has committed himself, he must carry it through.
5. The pastor must never take sides and be caught between contending parties. It must never be a personal matter with him.
6. Every act of discipline must be dealt with as quietly and as quickly as possible. The problem should never be discussed with those who are not concerned.
7. Finally, the pastor should try mild forms of discipline at first. The weak, erring brother should never be suspended if an admonition is all that is necessary.

Though all this, the shepherd ministers faithfully and works diligently to keep the sheep in the fold. Only in rare cases is it necessary to disfellowship and put one out of the church. Once this is done, the sheep is lost and the pastor's ability to help him is finished. As long as he is attending church and sitting in the pew there is a possibility that he might be helped and saved. A backslider can repent and be restored, but not outside of the church. His only hope is to stay in the church. For that reason, the shepherd will keep him in the fold regardless of the heartache and anxiety he is suffering because of the spirit of rebellion and disobedience manifested.

In a revival church, the back door seldom swings open. There is no exodus. The front door opens wide to admit all kinds of people burdened with guilt and problems. Here they find Jesus who lifts their burdens and enter the sanctuary to pray, worship and remain.

CHAPTER
TEN

PREACHING GOD'S WORD

"Preach the Word ..." (II Timothy 4:2)

There is a vast difference between preaching the Word and preaching about the Word. Preaching about the Word may impress the audience with the learning and eloquence of the preacher. This type of preaching may entertain, but it does not accomplish the desired result.

Impressing the hearer is not good enough. The minister preaches the Word in order to save souls, not to entertain them. He may have a vocabulary which uses thousands of difficult words and be as eloquent as Apollos but still not be preaching the Word. When he pronounces the benediction, the congregation may get into their cars to return home with the report that they heard a great oration. However, if it did not accomplish the desired result, the preacher has failed in preaching the Word. After a certain church service, a lady was commenting regarding the wonderful sermon she had just heard. "What a great sermon. My, how the preacher did preach this morning!"

She was asked by one who heard her, "What was the message about, and what was the preacher's text?"

"Now just a moment. What was it? I am afraid I have forgotten the text and really can't tell you the subject. But my, it was a powerful sermon. The preacher really preached!"

This type of impression needs no further comment. The preacher really did not preach. All he did was deliver an oration, not a message.

There is a truth here that should always be remembered. The message preached is equal to the message received. The preacher is simply delivering a message from the Lord to the people. If the audience does not receive anything, the preacher has not preached anything. The sermon can be judged correctly by what the hearers take home with them after the service.

The purpose of preaching is to save them that believe.

"For after that in the wisdom of God the world by wisdom knew not God, it pleased God by the foolishness of preaching to save them that believe" (I Corinthians 1:21). To the world, preaching is foolishness. But to those who are saved, it is the means by which the truth is planted in their hearts, bringing faith and salvation. Preaching the word is never foolishness and should never be looked upon lightly, neither by the preacher or the congregation.

We can see the importance of preaching the Word by a statement found in Psalm 132:2, "*. . . For thou hast magnified thy word above all thy name.*" We know that salvation is in the name of Jesus. Remittance of sin is through the name of Jesus. There is no salvation apart from it. However, here we find the Psalmist stating that the Lord has magnified his word above His name. This certainly shows us the importance of preaching the Word. Without it, His name would be ineffective to save the sinner. If the name of Jesus is great and powerful, God's Word is that much more. The name of Jesus is only as powerful as His Word.

There are three main results accomplished by preaching the Word:

1. It is the basis of faith. *"So then faith cometh by hearing, and hearing by the word of God" (Romans 10:17).* The preaching of God's Word builds faith and sows in the sinner's heart faith that he might believe to receive from the Lord all that was purchased for him on Calvary's cross. The Word of God is a source of faith. God's Word cannot fail; if

God said it, it will be.

2. Cleansing and sanctification. *"Now ye are clean through the word which I have spoken unto you" (John 15:3). "Sanctify them through thy truth: thy word is truth" (John 17:17).* Those who listen to God's Word being preached are being separated from the world, lifted up above the filth and degradation of sin, and set apart to serve the Lord. God's Word has the power to do this.
3. God's Word is a seed that is sown in the heart of man that brings the new birth. *"Being born again, not of corruptible seed, but of incorruptible, by the word of God, which liveth and abideth forever" (I Peter 1:23).* Before a birth takes place, there must be conception. In both natural and spiritual birth, seed has to be planted. Salvation is not produced by the seed of man, but by the incorruptible seed which is the Word of God. By preaching the Word, the seed is sown into the heart of an individual. If that heart contains fruitful, fertile soil, the seed will germinate and spring up to life eternal.

The minister preaches the Word of God in order to have definite desired results. Never does he preach just to have an eloquent sermon and receive the praise of men. He preaches to reach the souls of men, to bring sinners to the foot of the cross in repentance, and to build faith in their hearts to believe for the salvation of their souls. He preaches to the church to edify and encourage the saints. He preaches to the body of Christ that each child of God may separate himself from the elements of this world and be ready for the coming of the Lord. As he is preaching for results, he himself must have a burdened heart for the congregation, filled with love for each of them and believing God for the desired results.

A young man preached in a certain pulpit for several weeks without any results. Finally, he spoke to an older preacher and said, "Brother, I have been preaching for several weeks and have not seen any results. Not one soul has come to the Lord."

The older minister said to the young man, "When you preached, did you believe that you would have results?"

"No, I am afraid I did not."

"There's your problem. If you believe and expect results, then you will have them."

The young preacher took the advice of the older man and asked God to give him faith. His ministry was completely transformed. It was not just mechanical preaching, but now it was preaching that was anointed by the Holy Ghost. Fervent and motivated with real faith, the young man's heart was filled with joy as he began to see young men and women respond and come to the altar.

Results are always sure when the minister preaches God's Word with a burden, love, faith and the anointing of the Holy Spirit.

CHAPTER
ELEVEN

THE VOICE OF GOD

"Now then we are ambassadors for Christ, as though God did beseech you by us: we pray you in Christ's stead, be ye reconciled unto God' (II Corinthians 5:20).

God certainly desires to speak to His people. He wants His children to hear His voice and listen carefully to what He has to say to them. It is evident from the testimony of the Scriptures and personal experience that He uses several means in allowing His voice to be heard. According to the conditions and circumstances of the moment, He speaks through the following various means:

1. Directly. There are times when He speaks to an individual either by an audible voice or by a deep impression. The Bible gives many examples where God spoke audibly. Upon the road to Damascus, God spoke to Saul in an audible voice, *"Saul, Saul, why persecutest thou me?"* Then men who were travelling with Saul heard the voice but saw no man. In this manner, God can still speak to men.

   However, He may speak with a deep impression, an inward voice, which may be just as clearly heard as if it were shouted. In this matter, God has spoken to me clearly and emphatically. At times I even heard the words which He said. When God speaks, He will not leave us in doubt concerning the message He desires to communicate.

2. Prophecy. At Antioch, the Holy Ghost said, *"Separate me Barnabas and Saul for the work whereunto I have called them" (Acts 13:2).* God spoke here either through a message in tongues followed by an interpretation or through prophecy. At any rate, God spoke by means of a supernatural utterance of the Holy Ghost.

   God frequently speaks to the church by one of the gifts of utterance. At such times, the church should listen attentively to what God has to say.

3. Word of God. This is the final authority on all spiritual and eternal matters. Unchanging and infal-

lible, it provides the answer to every problem. It can never be questioned. As such, it is God's Word. When preached under the anointing of the Holy Spirit, it is the voice of God to all who listen.

4. God's Minister. The minister is preaching in Christ's stead. He is God's ambassador, delivering God's message. One should never minimize the importance of hearing the gospel preached by an anointed messenger expounding the truth of God's Word.

However, is the voice of the preacher the voice of God? Certainly not because the preacher is not God. Although the message he preaches is the infallible truth of God's Word, he himself is not infallible. He is still a man, an human being, subject to all the weaknesses of the flesh.

Upon one occasion, the people shouted that Herod's voice was that of a god. Because he accepted their acclaim and denied it not, he was eaten with worms and died. The reason was he gave not God the glory (Acts 12:23).

It is an indisputable fact that preachers do make mistakes. They have been known to make wrong statements and err in judgments. They may be men of God, ambassadors, speaking in Christ's stead, but they are still human. Anointed vessels through which God is speaking, certainly, but still human.

One of the great qualities needed here is humility. The more humble they are, the more they can be used of God to be His spokesman.

Even though they are not infallible and possess much humility, they can still preach with authority as Jesus taught (Mark 1:22).

How can a minister preach with authority even though he is conscious of his own human lack? How can he be humble and bold at the same time? In answering this, one must remember that he will be anointed in direct ratio to his broken, surrendered spirit. He must be yielded to be used by God. He is very much aware that he is a human, but he is bold because he is preaching God's message. Confidence is the key word here. He has prayed and heard from God. He is positively assured that he has heard and received the message that God wants him to deliver. Therefore, he confidently preaches with authority.

He preaches neither apologetically nor arrogantly. There is no argumentative tone to his voice nor a spirit of paternalism demonstrated. He does not preach down to the people nor does he preach at the people. As God's ambassador with God's message he addresses the congregation and ministers to them on a one to one basis.

When he stands behind the pulpit, he never humiliates anyone with sarcasm or ridicule. I have heard some ministers make remarks which have made me cringe. One minister who was dealing with evolution said to the church, "The only monkey you will see is when you look at yourself in the mirror." Ouch! It was not funny. With such a remark, the minister hurt himself more than anyone else.

The true minister of God ministers to his flock. He loves and is interested in the welfare of everyone. He values each man and woman, boy and girl, saint and sinner. His desire is to help, encourage and save. He uplifts and strengthens with God's Word. As such, He is God's ambassador preaching in Christ's stead the words of life eternal.

CHAPTER
TWELVE

THE MINISTRY OF LISTENING

"... But be gentle with all men, apt to teach, patient, in meekness instructing those that oppose themselves ..." (II Timothy 2:24-25).

One evening as I lay upon a hospital bed in Penticton, British Columbia, the cancer specialist came to my bedside and began to give me some instructions. As he talked I tried to enter into the conversation. The doctor very abruptly said, "I am doing the talking, and you are doing the listening." After this rebuke, I allowed him to do so.

The sheep know their shepherd's voice. It is the shepherd who talks and the sheep who listen. Are the sheep never allowed to talk? Certainly, there is a time when they can do so and upon such occasions, the shepherd listens. Chiefly, it is in counseling sessions that the sheep do the speaking.

People are human beings and battle with loneliness, discouragement, heartache and fear. Each person is an individual with his own problems and fears. He needs to have his problems solved with his burden lifted. However, before the pastor can minister to him, he must understand the problems that need to be solved. This can never be done successfully without the ministry of listening.

We must never treat lightly the problem of the saint who needs help. I have often listened to problems being expressed and confessed that they seemed trivial. They were so insignificant that I could have laughed at the thought that they were being considered as problems. However, the thing that always must be remembered is that although they seemed small to me, they were no small problem to the person who was burdened down with them. To the bleeding sheep, the matter was significant, and the sheep was hurting.

Counseling is time consuming. Many hours may be spent in the ministry of listening. Although it may take much time, the time may be invested most effectively. In the counseling session, the hurting and bleeding sheep may be helped more than at any time.

Upon more than one occasion I have patiently listened to saints who have confided in me their problems and troubles. At the close, I might give them a few words of advice and a word of prayer. They leave with a hearty handshake saying, "Pastor, you have been such a blessing to me. You have really helped." Actually, I have said very little. All that I had done was listen to them as they poured out their hearts. However, as they talked and confided in me, it was marvelous therapy. Their wounds were being healed as they unloaded their burdens.

Before souls can be won, they first must be reached. Souls are won on a one to one basis. They go to church and listen to their minister because they feel that their minister cares for them. He proves that he cares by patiently listening to them when they come with problems. He has the ability to help because he has built confidence. The confidence and trust earned allows him to communicate. Communication is not just a one way street. To communicate, a minister must be able to both talk and listen.

The shepherd who listens must never be surprised at what he hears. Sometimes, he may be shocked, but he must never let it be seen. He must never be critical or cynical. Patiently with loving understanding he listens. Then he counsels always with the welfare of the Christian at heart.

The shepherd who listens must always remember that

the one who is confiding and confessing to him in doing so because he has confidence in him. That confidence must never be betrayed.

A young sister confessed to her pastor of a besetting sin in her life. She was battling with an habit that was bringing guilt into her life. The pastor made a joke of it and spread the story throughout the church. It can be understood why the girl left the church, never to return. Such betrayal of confidence is tragic and unworthy of any true man of God.

May the sheep speak? Certainly, but never in rebellion nor in criticism of their shepherd. Sheep must never speak to sow seeds of discord and dissension in the flock. When they are guilty of such action, they must be firmly disciplined and silenced. God has stated that He hates the person who sows discord among the brethren (Proverbs 6:19).

There are many reasons why it is profitable for the shepherd to listen to the sheep occasionally:

1. The shepherd by listening is able to discern the spiritual welfare of each one and is then able to minister effectively according to the need.
2. The shepherd is able to discover the potential ability in each member of the flock. When he knows their interest, burden and ability, he can harness it for the upbuilding of the kingdom of God.
3. Not only does the shepherd become acquainted with the spiritual needs of each member, he becomes aware of any problems within the body itself. He is

able then to deal with anything that is festering before it develops into a major problem.

4. By having the privilege of speaking, the laymen may be able to contribute much to the church. Many laymen have much to offer in the way of business, administration and building ability. These talents must never be disregarded but used for the work of God. If the shepherd never listens to the sheep, he may be wholly unaware of the great contribution that can be made to the work of God.
5. Sometimes the sheep can even teach their minister deep truths. Every teacher must be willing to be taught. Anyone who is unteachable disqualifies himself from being a teacher. Let me illustrate this from my own experience.

I began preaching the gospel in the fall of 1936. At that time, I did not believe the new birth message. I preached that everyone who believed was ready for the rapture of the church.

During the war years, I pastored a large country church in eastern Ontario. This church was one of the oldest churches in Canada. I had in this church precious saints who had the Holy Ghost more years than I was of age. One morning, I was teaching the Bible class, and the question of the wedding garment came up. We entered into considerable discussion regarding who was ready for the coming of the Lord. I told them that every believer was ready. They did not refute me, but they gently and lovingly began to ask questions and quote Scripture. They slowly and gently backed me up into a corner where I knew that I had no further answer. I went home determined to find out what the Word of God had to say. I went through the entire New Testament and wrote out in my own handwriting every verse of Scripture that was dealing with salvation. When I finished, I changed my doctrine. God gave me that day a revelation regarding the new birth. Since then, my Bible teaching regarding the new birth has been circulated around the world.

Many times I have thanked God that on that Sunday morning I had listened to the voice of the sheep. If I had quenched their voice and silenced them, God could never have led me on into deeper truth.

6. By listening to the sheep, a good relationship between the pastor and the church members can be developed and maintained. This is also true in the home and family. When major decisions should be made, it is wisdom on the part of the father to allow each member of the family to speak and to give their thoughts concerning the matter. It might be regarding where they are going to go on the summer vacation. Mother has a preference and the children do also. The father allows them to voice their opinion. But when it is finished, the father makes the decision, and the whole family rallies around the decision that he makes. So it is in the church family.

There is no harm done in allowing the sheep to speak if they do not do it to contradict or rebel against their pastor. The pastor listens and then makes the decision. After it is made by the shepherd, then the entire flock rallies around that decision and unites to follow the leadership of the man of God whom God has placed over them.

There certainly is a time to speak, and there is a time to listen.

CHAPTER
THIRTEEN

THE MINISTRY OF COOPERATION

"And the servant of the Lord must not strive ..." (II Timothy 2:24).

There are some people who love to fight. They never seem to be content unless they are having a fuss with someone. Unfortunately, this same carnal spirit is sometimes manifested in the ministry. This should never be. The Apostle Paul wrote to Timothy exhorting him to be gentle unto all men. The true shepherd is going to be gentle with the sheep. He will not be guilty of dealing with them in a rough manner.

The minister's mannerism, attitude, spirit and even tone of voice in which he ministers may make the difference between success and failure. When the pastor speaks to his congregation in a belligerent tone, there is surely going to be a reaction.

When the child of God makes his way to the place of worship, he is undoubtedly weary in body and spirit. He has been battling traffic and fighting deadlines all day. He has encountered his share of stress and pressure and is looking forward to the rest and strength awaiting him in the presence of the Lord. The church is an oasis in the desert, a quiet haven of peace in the midst of a turbulent world.

What a disappointment when the peace of God is lacking. What a disillusionment when there is contention and confrontation, arguing and bickering instead of unity and harmony.

The pastor is the leader and sets the tone for all that transpires in an assembly. It is an easy matter to lay the blame elsewhere. If one wants to find a scapegoat, there is always one at hand. However, the person who is primarily responsible for the spirit that prevails in the assembly is the pastor. If he displays a spirit of belligerence and confrontation, this will be the attitude displayed by the members. However, such a spirit should never be found in the ministry. The true spirit of the servant of God is the man of peace who will not fuss and argue with anyone.

The minister is not interested in winning arguments but in winning souls. It is possible to win the argument but loose the soul. Argument or souls. Which will it be?

Gentleness and patience are not signs of weakness. The minister can be a solid as the rock of Gibraltar and lead with firmness and strength but in a spirit of kindness and love.

Sometimes the minister is inclined to interpret a difference of opinion as an attack upon his authority. He may look upon it as a threat and challenge to his leadership. Generally, this is a mistake. When matters of different opinions arise, he can ask God for wisdom. The Lord will never fail him. He must remember that those saints are people who can think for themselves and should be given the privilege of expressing their opinions if they do it in the right attitude and spirit.

It would be good if we would examine the wisdom shown by one of the apostles at a time of confrontation. The story is given in Acts chapter six where a complaint was brought to them regarding the Grecian widows. It was claimed that these widows were neglected. To what extent they really were is something that will never really be known. These Grecians had come from abroad, and they were used to more. It would be more difficult to satisfy them than the Hebrews who had always lived there.

When this complaint was brought to the apostles, there was no great confrontation. The apostles did not rebuke the Grecians for their murmuring but showed great wisdom in dealing with the whole matter.

They instructed them to choose seven men of honest report, full of the Holy Ghost and wisdom who would be appointed over the ministering of the tables. The apostles gave the qualifications, but the people themselves chose these seven men. After the selection was made, the apostles ordained them. It is interesting to note that the first seven deacons chosen were all Grecians. The apostles did not interpret this as a threat or challenge to their authority. They handled the situation wisely, and unity and harmony remained in the church.

There may be moments when the pastor will find that some of his people will disagree with him concerning some decisions that he has made. In such a moment, instead of carrying it through to great argument with some people becoming upset and angry, the minister should just back away from it and let the matter rest for a few days. Then he may bring it up again, approaching it from a new direction. It may be necessary for him to do this several times, but never at any time is there strive and contention. Finally, if he presents his cause carefully and wisely, the time will come when the brethren who are disagreeing with him will make a decision exactly as he desires. Sometimes, they themselves feel that it may be their decision. In such moments, everyone is happy, and unity and harmony are preserved.

There is a rule that must be remembered. A minister

himself must never be caught in a situation where he himself is the issue. A shepherd will never lift a finger to defend himself. Let God fight his battles. If God cannot vindicate him, then his case is hopeless.

When it is a matter of truth or righteousness, the man of God will not bow nor yield under pressure. He will stand straight and tall for what is right. The welfare of the kingdom of God will always come first. He will fight for truth and holiness but will back away from any confrontation where it is a personal matter.

I can relate many stories where I completely backed off from situations where it was becoming personal. I have always tried to put the church first and hand it over to the Lord Jesus to take care of. There have been times when I have had brethren refuse to speak to me or shake my hand. At such moments, I left the matter with God. I never even told my wife about such incidents. I certainly would not permit myself to be brought down into some petty argument. I always endeavored to rise above it, and God has never failed me.

The closing words of Dr. Beacher on his death bed were these: "It is not theology; it is not controversy; it is to save souls." To this we can all say amen.

CHAPTER
FOURTEEN

THE MINISTRY OF BEING EXPENDIBLE

"To the weak became I as weak, that I might gain the weak: I am made all things to all men, that I might by all means save some" (I Corinthians 9:22).

The successful shepherd of a flock will be completely, utterly abandoned to the will of God. Self interest will be laid aside. The work of God will always have first priority in his life. The welfare of the church will be uppermost in his mind and heart. He will recognize the cause as greater than he and it demands his best. A second best will never be good enough.

The minister's success will always be in direct ratio to his dedication. If self interest is motivating him, his effectiveness in ministering to others will be only ordinary. If always he is asking himself what is in it for me, he will remain mediocre in his outreach to others.

He must place himself irrevocably upon the altar of sacrifice. Not only does he make himself as being available to God, but he recognizes himself as being expendable. He is both. Sometimes it causes the minister of the gospel great sacrifices to do the will of God.

The reply of King David to Araunah should be the testimony of every faithful shepherd, "*... Neither will I offer burnt offerings unto the Lord my God of that which doth cost me nothing ...*" *(II Samuel 24:24).*

Araunah freely offered his threshingfloor to David. However, David insisted on paying for it. Accordingly, he paid fifty shekels of silver for the site upon which he was to build an altar.

So many times we offer unto the Lord sacrifices of that which costs us nothing. However, it costs to be in the work of God. Sometimes, it costs our all.

In Matthew chapter thirteen we find recorded the parable of the treasure hid in the field. In order to buy the field, a man sold all that he had. After he had sold all, he was able to obtain the field to secure the treasure. The field is the world. In order to enter the field to find the treasure of saving souls, the minister must sell out.

The testimony of the Apostle Paul should always be kept in mind. He wrote the following to the church at Rome: *"So, as much as in me is, I am ready to preach the gospel to you that are at Rome also" (Romans 1:15).* "As much as is in me is" expresses complete, absolute dedication to God's will. This means that he is both available and expendable. The apostle was ready to preach in Rome. Even so, the true minister of the gospel is at all times ready. He is ready to use every occasion to preach, to witness, and to minister. Also, he is ready to die if necessary for the name of Jesus.

The consuming passion of his life will be to minister to others. Every talent, every ounce of strength, every minute will be channelled towards the supreme purpose of saving souls. Not only does this mean dedication, but it means discipline and work. God has no place in His kingdom for lazy preachers!

One of the greatest sermons I have ever heard was preached by Bishop Lawson in the church in Kingston, Jamaica. After the service, the young men crowded around him with the following question, "Bishop, how may I be successful in the gospel ministry?" I still remember Bishop Lawson's reply to the enquiry. His answer consisted of only one word: W-O-R-K! He told these young men that under his ministry he had seen developed one of the largest congregations in New York City. It all came about because he worked.

Success does not just happen through wishful thinking. Revivals do not come to the church by just waving a magic wand. There is a price that must be paid. Revival is possible in every church that comes through fasting and prayer, complete dedication to God and W-O-R-K!

Bishop and Sister W.T. Witherspoon from Columbus, Ohio visited Jamaica upon three occasions. While there, they testified that there were evenings when they returned home in Columbus that they would be so weary that they would be unable to climb up the steps into their home. They would have to sit on the steps and rest before entering their home. Why would they be so weary? There is only one answer. This dedicated couple knew what it was to give their all and to work. As a result, they saw one of the largest Jesus name works in the world established in Columbus at that time.

I once heard of a Baptist preacher in the city of Vancouver, British Columbia who had a goal in his visitation program of making seventy five housecalls each week. In my fifty two years of ministering, I have never even come close to that. However, when I heard of a Baptist minister doing this, the desire was awakened in my heart. Dear Lord, may this Pentecostal preacher do better than that for Thee. Let no minister of another church do better than what I can do in the kingdom of God. It is not just making house calls, but it is in prayer, hospital visitation, and hours spent in counselling men and women. This all takes much effort. The work of the kingdom of God is not child's play; it calls for the strength of seasoned preachers of the gospel.

In the mind of every physician, the welfare of the patient always comes first. Likewise, the welfare of the flock will always come first in the mind of the shepherd. The shepherd who loves his flock will never complain about the effort and time expended in ministering to the sick and weak saints. The lambs must be nourished, fed and protected. The welfare of the sheep comes first. To this end, the shepherd has dedicated himself to be both available and expendable.

CHAPTER
FIFTEEN

THE MINISTRY OF COMPASSION

"But a certain Samaritan, as he journeyed, came where he was: and when he saw him, he had compassion on him" (Luke 10:33).

The priest and Levite saw the man lying in the ditch, naked and wounded. Undoubtedly, they had some pity for the man but did not offer to help. The good Samaritan came where the man lay and ministered to him. What made the difference was that the Samaritan had compassion. It was compassion that caused him to bind up the wounds and place him upon his donkey. It was compassion that would not permit him to pass by like the priest and Levite. A measure of pity was not sufficient; they lacked compassion.

Compassion is a deep feeling of sympathy and understanding! It is more than feeling sorry. It causes one to see himself in the same condition. It stirs the depth of one's soul to understand the need of the wounded and bruised. It compels the compassionate heart to pour in the wine and oil and bind up the wounds.

Out in the world, there are millions who are hurting. They are the swindled, betrayed and defrauded. They are the people who have been mistreated, abused and misused. They are the oppressed, exploited, and cheated. There fallen in the ditch of sin are the used and addicted. As the minister of the gospel goes to them with the words of life, he must be consumed with the spirit of Christ and be filled with the spirit of compassion. Without it, his ministry will be cold and barren. Like the Levite, he will only look and pass by on the other side.

The good Samaritan is Jesus Christ. As He looked over Jerusalem, he wept and was moved with compassion for the fainting multitude (Matthew 9:36). This means that his heart was stirred and aroused with sympathy and understanding. The spirit of Christ is such a spirit.

Jesus is still the same today. When we go to Him with our bruises and heartaches, He is stirred with compassion. "For we have not an high priest which cannot be touched with the feeling of our infirmities; but was in all points tempted like as we are, yet without sin" (Hebrews 4:15). What does it mean by saying that Jesus is touched with the feeling of our infirmities? Does it not mean that He is moved with compassion, that his heart of love is stirred with understanding to the degree that He can feel for us? Yes, when we are hurting, when we are tempted, and when we have fallen, our High Priest feels for us and is moved with compassion for us.

If there is any quality that the true shepherd needs above all others, it is compassion. There is far too much professionalism in the ministry. The preacher may perform the part of the minister but leave his congregation untouched and unmoved. Before he can move his audience, he must first be moved himself. Before the people can be touched with God's spirit, the preacher must be touched with compassion.

It would seem that the best training school for developing compassion is that of experience. If the minister has previously walked through valleys of discouragement, he can feel for those who are in similar dark valleys. If he has been rejected, he can have understanding for those who are being rejected. If he has had tragedy in his life and has suffered the loss of loved ones, he finds it not difficult to have compassion on those that are brokenhearted.

In November of 1985, I lay for twenty days upon a hospital bed in Penticton, British Columbia. When the doctor told me that I had cancer, I could not believe it. I had prayed for scores of others who were afflicted with cancer. I had officiated at the funerals of others who had died with cancer. It always happened to others, but it would never come my way. So I thought. Until the doctor shook me with his announcement. Throughout my stay in the hospital, my heart was filled with a song of deep thanksgiving. It was quite unexplainable. After being discharged, I examined the reason for the joy that I had experienced. The answer was that Jesus had permitted me to go through surgery so that I might have compassion for those lying upon hospital beds.

However, is this necessary? Not when the spirit of Christ fills the heart of God's minister. The spirit of Christ is the spirit of compassion. Filled with the Holy Ghost, the true shepherd finds it not difficult to identify with the sheep in all the different experiences of life. He can weep when they weep, laugh when they laugh, shout when they shout, rejoice with them in moments of victory and feel for them in times of suffering. At all times, compassion will cause him to reach out a helping hand to the man or woman in the ditch who has fallen among thieves.

Sheep love the shepherd who ministers to them not in the cold letter of the law but in the realm of the Spirit with deep feelings of compassion.

CHAPTER SIXTEEN

THE MINISTRY OF MINISTERING

"But watch thou in all things, endure afflictions, do the work of an evangelist, make full proof of thy ministry" (II Timothy 4:5).

Why do some preachers fail? Why do some grow discouraged and quit? The answer may be found in either one of these two reasons:

1. The preacher is frustrated because he is out of the will of God. He is trying to do something which he is not called to do. The pastor without a call will be frustrated and defeated. The tragic result of this is

that inevitably the pastor will give vent to his frustration over the pulpit and unload it upon the people.

2. The preacher has a wrong concept of the ministry. He cannot see the ministry as that of serving. His idea of a minister is standing behind the pulpit to a large appreciative audience.

Certainly the pastor does minister when the Word of God is preached; however, this is only part of it. Some of the most effective ministering is done on a person to person basis. It is the personal touch that generally brings the desired response.

At the First Church Council, James declared that God visited the Gentiles. He was able to take from them a church which bears His name because he came where they were. In every assembly wherc there is a move of God's spirit, God is visiting that assembly. Wherever and whenever God blesses, He stretches out His hand to touch and uplift. He reveals Himself personally.

Should we expect any difference in the ministry of the shepherd who cares for his sheep? No, at all times he will go to them where they are that he might minister to them personally.

Every pastor knows the experience of walking hospital corridors and entering hospital wards to minister to the sick. However, the ministry of ministering is not limited to the church sanctuary or the hospital ward. It might take place in the kitchen, the shop, the store, the hay field or the barn.

The alert pastor will never lack opportunities to minister to the needy. He will find needs everywhere, both spiritually and materially. On every hand, there will be people who will be in need of encouragement and uplifting.

In the church there may be a family that is destitute. The pastor may need to find some assistance and have a grocery shower for that family. He may need to assist the family from being evicted from their home or find another apartment for them. The question might be asked is this ministry? Certainly! When the pastor becomes a friend that stretches out a helping hand to encourage, he is their minister.

During the war years, I pastored a country church. The farmers were finding it difficult to find men to help them in the harvest. One man was in need of assistance. He was not a Christian nor did he attend any church. But, I offered to help him harvest his hay, working beside him for several days. During the time, I said very little regarding his need for salvation. Was I ministering to him? I certainly was! That fall, I had the joy of seeing that farmer make his way to that altar, kneel at the foot of the cross and weep his way through to victory. I would like to think that I had a part in that as I worked in his hay field.

In the north country where we began our ministry, we lived twenty five miles from the nearest doctor and hospital. During the winter the roads were all snowbound. No car could get through. But during those winter months, mothers would be giving birth.. My wife would attend them and be a midwife assisting them in birth and nursing them for a few days following. Was this ministering? It certainly was! We had the joy of seeing many of these people attend our services and some of them in our altars.

Ministering is reaching out with a tender touch of love, relieving the aches and pains, and binding up the broken-hearted. Ministering is extending to people a helping hand, letting them know that they are being loved. I shall never forget the tender touch of my mother as she would bathe my burning body when I was ill with scarlet fever. Night after night when she should have been asleep in bed, she was watching over and ministering to her sick boy. This is a true demonstration of the ministry of ministering.

People are longing to be understood. All around us are the lonely and discouraged. They are hungering for the kind word of a loving friend who can understand and uplift them. Here is where the pastor enters in. Next to Jesus Christ Himself, the pastor should be the best friend that anyone could have in this world. Many times the pastor's ministering may come before that of wife or husband, mother or father. That pastor, knowing the needs of each one, can reach out with a touch of tender kindness and lift them towards Christ.

CHAPTER
SEVENTEEN

THE MINISTRY OF SUBMISSION

"Obey them that have the rule over you, and submit yourselves" (Hebrews 13:17).

The spirit of pride and rebellion must never be found in the heart of the minister. Arrogance has no place in the heart of the true man of God.

One of the great characteristics of a successful pastor is humility. God will use a humble vessel but will refuse the proud and arrogant. *"Humble yourselves in the sight of the lord, and he shall lift you up" (James 4:10). "... The sacrifices of God are a broken spirit: a broken and a contrite heart, O God, thou will not despise" (Psalm 51:17).*

The humble pastor is a man who is approachable. The saints will feel free to go to him with their problems, and they will feel comfortable in his presence. On the other hand, they will feel rejected and uncomfortable approaching a man with a proud spirit. Their hearts will be full of fear and uneasiness. They will hesitate before opening their hearts to a proud person.

The Word of God teaches that the saints should obey their pastor. *"Obey them that have rule over you, and submit yourselves" (Hebrews 13:17).* It is very important here to remember that the minister is the first partakers of the fruits (II Timothy 2:6). An example is a powerful teacher. Children learn by what they see more than by what they are told. Likewise, the saints will follow the example set by their pastor. What they witness will leave a greater impression upon them than what they hear preached.

It is useless to teach the saints to obey their pastor if he in return has no respect for his presbyters and District Superintendent. If the minister criticizes his presbytery and rebels against the leadership over him, he had better keep quiet as far as telling his saints to obey him. All that he says to them will be in vain.

The spirit in these last days is rebellion and disobedience. This spirit of the anti-Christ should always remain in the world. It should never be brought into the church.

How beautiful to see a minister demonstrate a broken spirit of submission, obedience and respect. How beautiful it is to see an entire congregation of saints, in perfect harmony, following the examples set before them and demonstrating the spirit of submission and respect.

A word of caution might be noted here. Humility and submission are not signs of weakness. They reveal strength of character and Christian faith. Generally the proud man is the weak one.

Arrogance is a sign of insecurity. The arrogant man always feels that he is on the defensive. Everything is interpreted as a challenge and threat to his position and authority. This is far from the case. The humble man who is at peace with his assembly, with himself, and with his God preaches with boldness and authority. He is relaxed and not tense. He is motivated with love for the saints and the Word of God. Therefore, he is able to direct and lead the flock with confidence from the position of strength.

CHAPTER EIGHTEEN

THE MINISTRY OF LEADERSHIP

"Neither as being lords over God's heritage, but being ensamples to the flock" (I Peter 5:3).

The main thought of this book, *Dear Pastor: If Sheep Could Speak,* is that the shepherd leads the sheep. The sheep follow him because they know his voice. The entire relationship between the shepherd and the flock is wrecked when he reverses this order. The sheep will refuse to be driven. When this is attempted, they will jump through every hole in the fence.

What a blessing it would be if pastors would learn that they are leaders. When driven, the sheep will scatter. When led, the sheep will unite behind the shepherd and follow him to fountains of cool waters.

It is God's plan that the shepherd leads the way. The church can never reach higher heights nor go further than that of her ministers.

There is a verse of Scripture that has significant bearing upon this great truth: *"The husbandman that laboureth must be first partaker of the fruits" (II Timothy 2:6).* The Apostle Paul wrote to Timothy that the farmer had the right to reap the firstfruits of the harvest. Applying this principle to the church, it would mean that the pastor has the right to reap of the financial income of a church. It is the pastor who has the responsibility of being the shepherd of the tithes; however, there is a secondary application that may be applied here. He must be the first partaker in all the activity and ministries of the church. In prayer, worship, tithing and giving, he leads the way. The shepherd of the flock is the leader, going before. He sets the example for all to follow.

The sheep will not pray if the shepherd does not pray.

The sheep will not tithe if the shepherd does not tithe.

The sheep will not worship if the shepherd does not worship.

The sheep will not faithfully attend church if the shepherd does not faithfully attend church.

The sheep will not study the Bible if the shepherd does not study his Bible.

The sheep will not submit to authority if the shepherd does not submit to authority.

If the pastor is independent and will not follow God ordained leadership, then he cannot expect the saint to do so.

In the ministry of leadership, the importance of example cannot be over emphasized. The saints will at all times have their eyes upon their minister. Several years ago, one pastor gave a strong appeal to give to Christmas for Christ rather than giving Christmas presents within their family. In the church, there were some that listened to this admonition and did exactly as he had requested. One family had several growing children. At that particular Christmas they had no presents. They were all willing to make the dedication and the sacrifice until one day they were at the pastor's home, and they were shown the expensive gifts that the pastor had given to each one of his children. It was such a shock and disapointment to the children of this particular family that it took a long time to lay it upon the altar.

It is a regrettable thing that many ministers do not possess the qualifications of being a good leader. The ministry of leadership is lacking in many churches. We may consider some qualifications of a leader:

1. He must be a man of faith: faith in God, in himself, and in the church and message he preaches.
2. He must be a man who inspires trust and confidence. If he is insecure, he will interpret everything as a threat. As a result, he will always be on the defensive. The saints soon loose confidence in such a man.
3. He must be a man of humility. He is not afraid of sticking his neck out and venturing out into new areas. He is not afraid to make mistakes. However, he is quick to recognize and confess mistakes and make the proper correction and if necessary, restitution.
4. He is a man who is willing to listen to others. He does not try to exalt or defend himself if he has been wrong in some judgment.
5. He is a man who must know where he is going. He has clearly spelled out goals and objectives before him.
6. He is a man who must know what he believes. When he is preaching he is not on the defensive. He will teach and preach with authority. He knows that he is preaching the truth and so has confidence in himself and in God's Word. He declares the truth with power and anointing. Understanding that sweat is not anointing and perspiration is not inspiration, he simply declares the truth clearly, with plain speech and simple words.

The God ordained leader in the church is not a lord over God's heritage. He is not a sergeant major who barks out orders. He is an example who goes before. He knows that he is serving God. It is the Lord who promotes and who also can demote. He leads his flock through the ministry of love and gives himself wholly, completely and unreservedly to the ministry of being all that God wants him to be as a leader among God's people.

CHAPTER NINETEEN

THE MINISTRY OF PATIENCE

"And let us not be weary in well doing: for in due season we shall reap, if we faint not" (Galatians 6:9).

Have you tried to help a rose bud unfold into a beautiful rose? You simply cannot wait for nature to take its course. So you unfold each petal one by one. What do you have when you are finished? A pitiful mess! The only thing you have succeeded in doing is destroying what would have been a gorgeous rose. If nature is allowed to take its own time the rose bud will effortlessly unfold into a beautiful bloom bringing pleasure to all who behold.

Have you ever tried to help a chicken out of a shell? Be careful and take your time for otherwise all you will have is a soggy dead chick in your hands.

There are many processes in this world which take time. Impatience will destroy and kill. Getting in a hurry only hinders rather than helps the desired end.

Of all the Christian graces, patience is one of the greatest. It is a quality that every Christian should possess but especially the minister of the gospel. A shepherd of God's sheep must have great patience. Without patience the pastor and missionary will fight frustration and discouragement. Under the pressures of ministry an impatient man will not have the strength to continue. He will simply quit.

We live in a push button age. In our homes arc microwaves and automatic appliances. We carry home from the supermarket instant puddings and ready made cakes. Does this streamlined modern age give us more time to pray, study our Bibles and enjoy our families? On the contrary spare time is becoming more and more a precious commodity. Life is a constant rush. So much so, that if a person is not careful it can develop into a panic resulting in nervous breakdowns and heart attacks. In the business world the pressure of meeting deadlines and quotas can become almost unbearable.

The spirit of this fast jet age must never take over in the ministry of the Holy Ghost preacher. He must never be caught up in the spirit of restlessness, uneasiness and dissatisfaction. Impatience is the quality that breeds this kind of spirit and must be fully eradicated.

Pentecostal altars are influenced by this modern spirit of impatience. Hurry up! Get it over with! We must get down to the restaurant for some fellowship. Fifty years ago new converts spent hours seeking for the Holy Ghost. Seldom was the altar service dismissed before midnight. One preacher declared that this was wholly unnecessary. The Comforter has come and all one has to do is to believe and receive. This is true and this fact cannot be challenged. But how long does it take to repent? One person may repent in a few minutes. The next person may take days to pray through. In the early thirties I remember lying on my back at the altar for hours seeking for the glorious infilling of the Holy Ghost. We recognize that it does not have to take hours but let us not get in a hurry. A shallow experience may be the result.

Too frequently we settle for forced births. Many evangelists are anxious to count numbers. One evangelist who preached a crusade in a church where I was pastoring was guilty of this. In this particular crusade many strangers visited the services. Under the persuasion of the evangelist they came to the altar. In a few minutes they were told by the evangelist that they had received the Holy Spirit. I can still see the disappointed expression on their faces revealing the disillusionment they experienced. Some of these visitors we never saw again.

The work of God takes time. Let us never get in a hurry. One well known minister whom I respect greatly made this statement in a district convention: "I can go into any town and have at least fifty converts baptized within six months." Although I respected this minister I recognized this as being an extravagant statement. In my own mind I said, "How I would like to take you to the states of Montana and Wyoming, and watch you do it. Please demonstrate for me."

Many times impatience is the direct result of goals which are not realistic. Such unrealistic goals insist that we must have revival NOW. We must reap the harvest TODAY. Otherwise we are a failure.

Some preachers remind me of a farmer who ploughs the field today. The next day he harrows the ground. The third day he is in the field with the seed drill. The fourth day he wants to enter the field with the combine to reap the harvest. The farmer knows that this is impossible. They have more common sense than some modern preachers.

It is God who gives the harvest and it is God who gives a revival. The one who ploughs and sows must learn to wait upon God whether he be farmer or preacher. There needs be no question about results. If the ploughing and seeding are properly done the harvest is certain.

"He that goeth forth and weepeth, bearing precious seed, shall doubtless come again with rejoicing, bringing his sheaves with him" (Psalm 126:6).

Patience produces perseverance. No matter what the results appear to be, the patient preacher never gives up. There is no place to quit in the work of God. If one is in the will of God the harvest is sure.

I have taught Pioneer Evangelism upon many occasions in Bible Colleges. In my classes I have told the students that it takes fives years to raise up a church congregation. Sometimes it is accomplished in five months. However, examine it closely. Generally when this happens there are a number of tentmakers accompanying the pioneer evangelist. Certainly if a small congregation moves into a town with him the results will be different. Also some preacher may have already been there ploughing and sowing the seed. In this case the evangelist moves into town and reaps the harvest.

I have been involved in Pioneer Evangelism since the fall of 1936 and do not consider myself a novice. In Jamaica during the first term the number of churches grew from eight to twenty-three. During six years in the Northwestern District while I was Superintendent there were twenty new churches opened.

I have witnessed pioneer evangelists raising up two or three congregations and losing them one by one before there is the joy of seeing a strong assembly established. A farmer may rejoice as he looks upon acres of wheat waving in the breeze. Then he is heartbroken as he watches the crop destroyed with a plague of grasshoppers. Next year it may be the frost and the next year a drought.

The farmer may witness two or three crop failures before he reaps the harvest for which he has been laboring. Why is he able to reap? It is because of patience.

"For ye have need of patience, that, after ye have done the will of God, ye might receive the promise" (Hebrews 10:36).

Wrong goals will cause a Christian, minister or saint, to become impatient and frustrated. The desire for crowds, applause, and recognition can be wholly destructive to a person's faith. Once a young pastor wrote me a heart breaking letter expressing his discouragement. "I did so much want to be a success."

It was a pitiful letter. So much so that I boarded a train and rode onc full night and day to visit him. I did my best to try to encourage him.

What is success? Crowds, spectacular reports, recognition, numbers? Is it not being in the perfect will of God and being faithful? It should be remembered that God keeps a different set of records. We are only a success when we fulfill God's divine purpose in our lives. To hear Him say, "Well done!" is what really matters. Certainly we can be just as successful preaching to a dozen souls as preaching to a congregation of several hundred.

Why is patience needed? It is because we are dealing with people. Every person is different, every church assembly is different, every town and community is different. The response differs according to the congregation.

In a congregation the preacher may be aware that there are people present who do not like him. He may also know that there are some who rebel against his teaching. How does this influence him? Does he preach differently? Does he become impatient, harsh, arrogant or negative? Not if he knows the meaning of patience. Although he may be fighting frustration and discouragement he will never allow this to show over the pulpit. There he preaches God's Word. He ministers to people, good and bad, spiritual and carnal. It is God's Word which will accomplish the work of grace in each heart. The minister must rise above all pettiness and feelings which would distract from God's Word.

The Bible has much to say about Patience:

"And not only so, but we glory in tribulations also: knowing that tribulation worketh patience; And patience, experience; and experience, hope:" (Romans 5:3-4).

"In your patience possess ye your souls" (Luke 21:19).

"But let patience have her perfect work, that ye may be perfect and entire, wanting nothing" (James 1:4).

The benefits of possessing patience are many. In one of his sermons John Wesley had this to say regarding patience:

"One immediate fruit of patience is peace: a sweet tranquility of mind; a serenity of spirit, which can never be found unless where patience reigns. And this peace often rises into joy. Even in the midst of various temptations, those that are enabled 'in patience to possess their souls', can witness, not only quietness of spirit, but triumph and exultation." Sermons on Several Occasions by John Wesley, 1855.

Much patience is needed in making disciples of new converts. Sometimes the learning process is slow. Being told a truth just one time generally is not enough. It takes time to train, teach and disciple in the development of spiritual saints.

It is inspiring to examine the patient training of an athlete or a musician. In 1934 while attending summer school in the city of Hamilton, Ontario, I boarded in a home next door to a musician. This young man was a gold medalist pianist. Day after day he practised on the piano from morning to night. As I listened to him I could readily understand why he was able to win gold medals and rewards.

While teaching mathematics at King's College in Vancouver a young man attended my classes. He had previously failed two times in Mathematics 91. He needed his Upper School Algebra in order to continue his college education. It was not just the regular classes I spent with him. We spent several hours in extra instruction after school and at noon hours. What satisfaction I had when I heard that he had passed the departmental examination in Mathematics 91.

Nevertheless there are preachers who show little patience with young converts. It is enough to tell them once! However, it is not enough! Over and over again they must be instructed and exhorted. Through patient perseverance the shepherd will eventually see the Christian blossom and develop like a beautiful rose.

What a shameful disgrace to see a mother scream at a little one who spills some milk! Slapping and swatting the baby accomplishes nothing except to reveal the mother's nasty temper. The ultimate result will be that the child will grow up to be impatient and to have a nasty disposition. The patient loving parent will see her offspring grow up to be a beautiful Christian.

The same principle holds true in the church. If the pastor is nasty and impatient with the sheep, if he scolds and speaks harshly, the sheep will either scatter, or they in turn will develop into unhappy people who fuss and fight. By faithfully ministering with love and patience it is possible to see the new converts become part of a strong, healthy, contented flock.

CHAPTER
TWENTY

THE MINISTRY OF LOVE

"... Simon, son of Jonas, lovest thou me? He saith unto him, Yea, Lord; thou knowest that I love thee. He saith unto him, Feed my sheep" (John 21:16).

Three times Jesus asked Peter, "Lovest thou me?" Three times Jesus instructed Peter to feed His sheep.

There are several truths which may be learned from this beautiful story.

1. If we love Jesus we shall also love God's children.
2. To show our love for Jesus we must minister to His

sheep.

3. We may minister to Jesus by ministering to His church.
4. To properly tend sheep we must first love the sheep.

It is difficult to deceive the flock with a feigned love. The sheep know whether the shepherd loves them. They know if his ministry is merely professional and motivated by self interests. Heart power can be felt. When he ministers from a heart full of love there will be a response. He does not need to tell them that he loves them. They will already know it. They also will know if his ministry is motivated by self interests only.

A good wife who loves her husband will spend hours preparing a meal. She will cook food that he enjoys. Her efforts will be to please the man she loves. Her reward is to see her husband eat well and enjoy his food.

Likewise the pastor who loves his flock will not feed them leftovers and warmed up hash. He will spend hours on his knees hearing from God and studying the Bible. It will not be that he might preach an eloquent oration. The effort is put forth because he loves his flock. Therefore he feeds them well. The preparation which goes into his messages will be directly proportioned to the amount of love he has for them.

An example of a preacher who only ministered because of carnal motives is a certain Bible teacher I once knew in one of our camp meetings. It was time for him to enter the tabernacle to speak to the crowd. He turned to another preacher and said, "Well, it is time for me to go in and say something to these birds."

What an insult to God's saints! What a confession from a man who is wholly ignorant of his calling! What a horrible tragedy!

Sometimes evangelists will spend the day sight seeing until it is almost church time. Then he grabs a message at the last minute on the run. What a disgrace! The people have come to church after a hard day's work expecting to hear a message from God. Instead they get a play back of a warmed up sermon which has already been practised upon congregations from Dan to Beersheba.

Love for the sheep must be real. It cannot be counterfeited. There is little difficulty in loving the precious lambs who have been brought into the fold under one's own ministry. The problem lies in loving the old sheep who have been in the church for years. They have been taught by previous pastors. Their ways are set and not likely to change easily. Can a pastor love those who are giving him difficulty?

Certainly. In a family it is the sick child or the wayward son who will receive the most attention and love. The straying sheep will need the most attention and eventually will receive the lost love.

How can a person love the unloving? How can a pastor

continue to love a person who refuses to respond? First of all, ask the Lord to baptize your heart with love. Jesus can fill your heart with love for the unlovable. Secondly, you learn to love by loving. You learn to swim by swimming. You learn to preach by preaching. You learn to love by loving. Begin to share and give of yourself. It will be amazing just how much love will flood your heart once you have started to love and care.

True love for the saints will be revealed in many ways. Time that is spent in sermon preparation, in visitation and counselling, will not be begrudged. The tone of the minister's voice will show what is in the heart. He will not speak roughly to the sheep. Even when it is necessary to rebuke it will be done with longsuffering (II Timothy 4:2).

"... the good shepherd giveth his life for the sheep" (John 10:11).

The shepherd who does not love the sheep will be quite unwilling to sacrifice for them. The shepherd who loves will be willing to die for his flock. He will be giving, sharing, and sacrificing all the way. The motivating power of this will be love.

He will consider no sacrifice too great. As a result there will be a beautiful reward. If the shepherd loves the sheep, he will be rewarded with their love. If he speaks, they will listen to his voice. If he leads they will follow. If he sacrifices they will sacrifice. If he is willing to die for them, they will be willing to die for him.

As a result the relationship which will develop between pastor and saints will be wholesome and beautiful. The assembly of the saints will be seasoned with precious unity and fellowship. There will be sweet harmony building a church which will experience a Holy Ghost revival. Such a church will grow, and grow, and grow!

CHAPTER
TWENTY ONE

THE MINISTRY OF STEWARDSHIP

"Moreover it is required in stewards, that a man be found faithful" (I Corinthians 4:2).

The pastor of a church is more than being a preacher. The pulpit ministry is possibly the most important part of his work, but it is not the only thing. The pastor must be a business manager, an accountant, a faithful steward. This book would not be complete without a chapter dealing with stewardship.

Who is a steward? A steward is a person who has been

entrusted with the goods of another. As he handles these affairs the interests of the other person must always come first.

Who are stewards? All of us. Everyone is a steward. We come into the world naked and we shall leave naked. Everything we are, have, or possess, comes from the Lord. Let us mention just a few: time, jobs, employment, money, finances, talents, skills, God's Word, and souls of men around us.

Faithfulness is the greatest characteristic of a good steward. A faithful steward will assume personal responsibility with no self interest. A faithful steward will have achieved self discipline. Every man is a steward and can be a faithful one. Faithfulness is a quality that every person may possess.

Sentiment and emotions motivate us and influence our decisions. However, faithful stewardship is not determined on the basis of sentiment. It is carried out on the basis of principle. We do not make mortgage payments or pay rent on the basis of our emotions but rather principle. The rent is due and we pay it whether we enjoy it or not. The good steward will do the right thing even though it means great personal sacrifice.

Although every man is a steward of some nature, it is especially true regarding the shepherd of the sheep fold. In his office of leadership he cannot avoid making far reaching decisions. He is responsible for the health and welfare of the assembly and one day he will be answerable to our chief shepherd Jesus Christ.

There are many things which have been trusted to the pastor's keeping. Let us first consider the matter of finance. The pastor must know how to handle money. It should be remembered that it is necessary for the progress and growth of every assembly. Money is not the root of all evil but the love of money is (I Timothy 6:10). Money may be a curse or a blessing. It may be our servant or our master. If we are its master then it becomes a blessing.

Money is simply a medium of exchange. If we hold on to it, it is worthless. It only has value when it is exchanged for something worthwhile. Money represents a person's time, energy, and skill. If a saint works on the job for ten dollars per hour, and places ten dollars upon the offering plate, he is giving to the Lord one hour of his life. The pastor should always remember this as he appeals to the church for donations to meet certain needs.

Good stewardship begins with a budget. The minister must have his own personal finances on a strict budget and also that of the assembly. In this way finances will always be under control. No N.S.F. checks will be written. The church's credit will always be healthy. All bills will be paid on time when they are due. All building and expansion programs will be carefully planned according to the budget.

It will be profitable to remember this little saying: "If

our outgo is greater than our income, Then our upkeep will be our downfall."

In any expansion program the pastor must know when to quit. Sometimes there is a thin line drawn between faith and presumption. It is wonderful to move forward and launch out within the limits of one's faith. However, there is no excuse for being presumptuous or fool hardy.

In any building program the mortgage should be financed so it can be paid by the present generation. It is actually sinful to mortgage our children and expect them to pay for our presumption. I have taught Church Building upon many occasions and have used a formula which I have gleaned from a Baptist text book. I believe that it is as good as any. Here it is:

1. Before starting to build have one-third of the budget needed;
2. During construction raise one-third of the total costs;
3. Finance no more than one-third of the total costs.

I have studied this closely and am persuaded that this is sound financing.

In two separate instances I have known of pastors leading their churches into expensive building programs which they could not afford. In each case the pastor resigned under pressure. In each case his successor had a nervous breakdown. This kind of poor management is needless and reveals irresponsibility upon the part of the pastor.

The responsibility of stewardship is not just in proper management in the handling of the church's assets, but also in the instruction of good stewardship given to the church.

In 1936 as I was leaving for the north country to preach the gospel, one of the elders of the local church said to me, "Ralph, do not forget to preach tithing. It is part of the gospel."

I have consistently tried to follow his advice. I have made it a policy to preach a message on tithing regularly each year. The saints will not tithe unless they are taught. A tithing church will be a church of revival. It is the pastor's place to lead the congregation in every aspect of good stewardship.

The minister must carefully keep his own finances under control. He should never forget that the borrower is servant to the lender (Proverbs 22:7). If he is under the pressure of heavy debts he can never do justice to the spiritual aspect of his ministry.

Stewardship involves more than finances. The pastor is a steward of the mysteries of God (I Corinthians 4:2) and the manifold grace of God (I Peter 4:10). This means that he cannot pick his sermons at random. He must conscientiously and prayerfully minister as the Holy Spirit would direct according to the need of the people. Just as there will be an accounting on financial stewardship he must also answer regarding how he handled the great truths of

God's Word.

There is only one thing God requires of a steward and that is faithfulness. This is not beyond his reach. He can be faithful. This places every saint and minister on the same level for the same is required of each. In the judgment day each may receive the same reward when Jesus says "WELL DONE" to each of his faithful stewards.

CHAPTER
TWENTY TWO

THE MINISTRY OF BEING A FATHER

"For though ye have ten thousand instructors in Christ, yet have ye not many fathers" (I Corinthians 4:15).

There is something lacking about a home when the father is absent. The mother may be an excellent mother and be very faithful and loving. Nevertheless it is not just the same without father. When he is away there is an empty place that only father can fill. There is a weakness in the very structure of the home without father. Father gives the home strength and stability that no one else can give it.

Likewise there is something lacking in the church assembly when the pastor is absent. It is simply not the same. The minister who is supplying in the pulpit may be a more eloquent preacher than the pastor but it still is not the same.

The presence of the pastor gives stability. All uneasiness and apprehension are gone when the pastor is at the helm. If he is merely sitting on the platform there is a quiet trust and peace that can be felt by everyone.

There is vested in the pastor authority and responsibility. These two qualities cannot be divorced one from the other. The man who shoulders the responsibility of leadership must also be given the authority which rightly belongs to his office. This authority cannot be demanded. It must be earned. It must be recognized by all, from the board of elders down to the children in the nursery.

The pastor should consult with his board of deacons concerning major decisions. However, when that final decision is made, right or wrong, it must be that of the man of God whom God holds responsible.

Responsibility for a flock of God's sheep is not a light thing. The hireling fleeth when danger comes but the shepherd stays and protects the sheep.

"The hireling fleeth, because he is an hireling, and careth not for the sheep" (John 10:13).

When there is a revival and souls are being born at the

altars, preachers are quite willing to take credit for the move of God. When there is a new convert won to Christ, everyone will believe that he had a share in winning the soul. Pastor and evangelist will both share in the good report.

On the other hand, who takes responsibility for the wandering sheep? Oh, they are just a bunch of backsliders and rebels. It is good riddance to see them gone. There is such blessed peace and unity now since the seats are emptied. Such is the reasoning of the hireling. But who is actually responsible? We should always remember that God will hold someone responsible for those wandering sheep out in the wilderness. The hireling will never be willing to accept the responsibility. Only the man of God who is the spiritual father to the assembly will be willing to accept the responsibility. Certainly someone will answer to God for the wandering sheep who are not in the fold.

The Pioneer Evangelist who has pioneered the church will never scatter the sheep. He has ploughed, harrowed, sown the seed and reaped the harvest. He has baptized the new converts and helped pray them through to the glorious baptism of the Holy Ghost. Such a man will give his life for the flock. When the ship Zion is rocked by angry storms he will remain at the helm. He will be the last to leave the ship. This pioneer preacher is the father to the flock.

Paul wrote to the Corinthian church that they might have

ten thousand instructors but there are few fathers. The instructors may preach and teach, but run when the hurricane roars. The father stands firm and refuses to run, yield, or compromise. He stands firm as the rock of Gibraltar.

It is no wonder that such a man can speak with authority. Jesus spoke not as the scribes but with authority.

"For he taught them as one having authority, and not as the scribes" (Matthew 7:29).

What a comfort to listen to the voice of the father! All is well when you hear the voice of authority.

After cancer surgery I lay in a bed in the hospital, in Penticton, British Columbia. One evening Dr. Chritchley, cancer specialist, came to my bedside. When he started to talk to me I started to reply. I shall never forget what he said to me. "I am doing the speaking; you are doing the listening."

Here was an authority on cancer speaking. I was quite willing to be quiet and do the listening.

When the father speaks with authority, the children had better be quiet and listen. When the pastor speaks with authority the sheep do well to listen. When the father of the flock speaks there is no need for the sheep to speak.

CHAPTER TWENTY THREE

DEAR JOE

Dear Brother Joe,

Greetings.

So you see, Joe, saints are not just puppets. They are members of the body of Christ. Both minister and layman are members of the same body, working together in beautiful harmony to further the work of God. Both have a vital part to play in the extension of Christ's kingdom upon earth. Both are only successful when they are content to fulfill the will of God in their lives.

Your pastor certainly is not a bully, a dictator, a lord over God's heritage. He is your shepherd watching over your soul knowing that one day he must give an account. His main concern is your welfare, temporal and spiritual. He desires to see you develop and be used by God at your fullest potential.

As your pastor, I invite you to maintain a trust and confidence in the leadership God has given you. I encourage you to keep a spirit of openness and frank communication. If you have questions which need to be answered, be quick to come to me with them.

Let me give you a final word of admonition. While we shall love each other and maintain a warm friendship, yet it must always be on the level of pastor and saint. Otherwise respect may be destroyed. We must never become so familiar with each other that there is no respect. You must not call me by my first name but address me as pastor. It is not because I am so high and lofty that I cannot be approached. You shall always be able to reach me and feel free to unburden yourself. I assure you that I shall always love you and have your interests at heart. However, respect must be maintained, not so much for me personally, but for the office I fill, and what that office represents.

I do trust that I have helped you. Be content in the place in Christ where the Holy Ghost has placed you. Both you and I shall then together make the rapture.

With Christian love — Pastor.

CHAPTER
TWENTY FOUR

DEAR PASTOR

Dear Pastor,

First of all, let me express to you my sincere appreciation for the time that you have taken with me. I shall never find words to thank you sufficiently. You have certainly changed my thinking concerning the ministry. It has been a revelation to me and I shall never be critical of them again.

You have pushed back the horizon of my understanding and allowed me to see the calling and work of the pastor in a brand new dimension. I begin now to comprehend somewhat the scope of the minister's responsibility. Henceforth I shall stand behind you and all the ministry with my fervent prayers.

Not only do I understand in a greater measure the office of the pastor but I have found my rightful place in the Lord. I assure you that never again will I feel like a non-entity, just a name on a church roll, a number on a ledger, a seat warmer. I can now recognize my rightful place in the body of Christ. I shall no longer feel throttled, and shall be free to speak when it is in order. While exercising my God given rights in the body I shall be quick to listen to the voice of my shepherd. Never shall I speak anything which would be of a derogatory nature.

I thank God for you, Pastor, who has shown me such understanding. By God's grace I dedicate myself anew to be a faithful saint, doing everything in my power to enhance the work of God, and to hold up the hands of the man of God who is my shepherd. If you continue to lead me as you have until now, I pledge to follow you, my shepherd, regardless of tempestuous winds, across the plains and through deep valleys, to the green pastures. My trust and confidence in you is such that I know you will lead me to the still waters and pastures green. I shall be content to abide in the sheep fold where you are the shepherd. May the Lord ever bless you, Pastor. I love you.

Joe.